A NEGRO EXPLORER AT THE NORTH POLE

A NEGRO EXPLORER AT THE NORTH POLE

THE AUTOBIOGRAPHY OF
MATTHEW HENSON

With a new Introduction by
S. ALLEN COUNTER
author of *North Pole Legacy: Black, White, and Eskimo*

INVISIBLE CITIES PRESS
MONTPELIER, VERMONT

Invisible Cities Press
50 State Street
Montpelier, VT 05602
www.invisiblecitiespress.com

Library of Congress Cataloging-in-Publication Data

Henson, Matthew Alexander, 1866–1955.
A Negro Explorer at the North Pole : the autobiography of Matthew
Henson / Matthew Henson ; with a new introduction by S. Allen Counter.
p. cm.
Originally published: New York : F. Stokes, 1912. With new intro.
ISBN 1-931229-00-7 (cloth : alk. paper) —
ISBN 1-931229-01-5 (paper : alk. paper)
1. Henson, Matthew Alexander, 1866–1955. 2. African American
explorers—Biography. 3. North Pole—Discovery and exploration.
I. Title.

G635.H4 A3 2001
919.804—dc21 2001016611

Manufactured in the United States of America

Book design by
Tim Jones for
Sterling Hill Productions

Special thanks to Verne Robinson for his invaluable help in putting together this edition.

FIRST EDITION

CONTENTS

INTRODUCTION TO THE NEW EDITION

Matthew Henson, an Extraordinary American

BY S. ALLEN COUNTER, D.M.Sc., Ph.D.

WHAT KIND OF MAN was Matthew Henson? In my many years of research on his life, perhaps nothing I have found better answers this question than a statement written in the April 1920 edition of *National Geographic* magazine by Admiral Donald B. MacMillan, which says, "And the Negro? He was indispensable to Peary and of more real value than the combined services of all four White men." MacMillan went on to say, "With years of experience equal to that of Peary himself, an expert dog driver, a master mechanic, physically strong and most popular with the Eskimos, talking the language like a native, clean, full of grit, he went to the Pole with Peary because he was easily the most efficient of all Peary's assistants."

Matthew Henson explored the Arctic for over eighteen years with naval officer Robert E. Peary. He made significant contributions to Arctic exploration and was, in Peary's own words, indispensable to the expeditions. Henson was a man of great pride and dignity. He was born in Maryland to a humble family of farmers. At about age seven he and his younger sister moved to Washington, D.C., to live with relatives after the death of his father. Young Matthew attended the local public school and, as was common in those days, completed sixth grade with a well-rounded basic education. He left school to take on some of the menial jobs that were available to African Americans in the latter part of the nineteenth century, but he had a strong desire to travel and see the world. This longing for travel and adventure led him to the seaport at Baltimore where he was hired as a cabin boy on a merchant ship. For over six years he sailed around the world, learning languages and trades, and developing into a versatile young man. When he met Robert E. Peary in Washington, D.C., in 1887 he had more seagoing experience than the ambitious young naval officer, who as a surveyor for the U.S. Navy had been mainly confined to a desk. Peary was immediately taken by this bright young man and said that it was because of Henson's experience and intelligence that he hired him as an assistant. Henson was equally impressed with Peary's intelligence, ambition, and the respect that he had shown him as an African American that made him "willing to offer him my services."

In 1909 Henson and Robert Peary were the first Americans to stand at the North Pole. They remained friends and collaborators until Peary's death in 1920. Nevertheless, Henson never received proper recognition for his contributions to Arctic exploration and the North Pole discovery. He died in 1955 a proud man, yet disappointed that his country never fully appreciated him. In 1947 Henson gained some celebrity when author Bradley Robinson wrote a biographic novel about his life entitled *Dark Companion.*

Robinson, the son of a member of the Explorers Club of New York City, had heard his father talk about a remarkable man named Matthew Henson on numerous occasions. The elder Robinson had shared with his son the club's belief that it was Matthew Henson who had made the North Pole discovery possible. Though Bradley Robinson was not a member of the Explorers Club, he interviewed several of the club's elder statesmen and learned that there was considerable evidence that Matthew Henson had essentially led the way from the base camp all the way to the North Pole.

Dark Companion was the second book about Matthew Henson's experiences and adventures over his many years of Arctic exploration with Robert Peary. The first book was written by Henson himself in 1912, and was entitled *A Negro Explorer at the North Pole* ("Negro" was the officially accepted term for African Americans or Blacks in the early 1900s). Henson had begun to give lectures in New York at schools and at African-American colleges in the East, and wanted a scholarly work to accompany his talks. He sought, and received, endorsement as a learned man in Black educated circles.

It is important to note that Henson was the only member of the expedition who was permitted to write a book about the North Pole discovery—a point that has been used by some of Peary's detractors as proof of his poor character and his failure to reach the Pole. Because of the competition for publicity and ownership of adventure in that era, Peary had an agreement with all of his men that they would not be permitted to write about or profit from the North Pole expeditions that he led. Anyone who has led an expedition understands Peary's rule in this regard. Then and now, individuals seeking fame and fortune can participate even marginally in exploration projects and return to claim exaggerated contributions and financial reward. Henson, however, was able to convince Peary that he would be writing for a largely Black constituency, which would in no way conflict with Peary's White readership in the strictly segregated America of 1909. Henson's book did in fact have a wide readership in America's Black communities. For his contributions to Arctic exploration and his writings, Henson was awarded honorary master's degrees from Morgan State College in Baltimore, Maryland, and Howard University in Washington, D.C., two of the preeminent Black educational institutions of that period. At Dillard University in Louisiana, a Matthew Henson Hall was dedicated in his honor.

There are numerous factors that make Matthew Henson a unique American. He must, however, be viewed in the context of his time. Imagine in 1887, a little more than twenty years after the abolition of American slavery, a young Black man in Washington, D.C., comes to know a young white naval officer who seeks his assistance in undertaking one of the great projects of their time, digging a canal—later to become the Panama Canal—that would link the Atlantic and Pacific Oceans. Henson, who had more experience in overseas travel than the young navy lieutenant who employed him, immediately established a rapport with Peary. In fact, he so impressed Peary with his all-around skills that Peary described him as having "greater than average intelligence and pluck." When they returned from Nicaragua in 1888, their relationship had become so close that Henson referred to Peary as his "friend" in all of his letters. Needless to say, a friendship between a Black man and a White man in 1888 was not common, and was indeed quite unusual. It was also unusual for a Black man to have steady employment in that era, outside of essentially feudal agrarian or servant labor. But because Peary saw in Henson someone who could be of considerable benefit to him in his quest for greatness, he offered Henson a position as messenger in the Navy shipyard of Philadelphia. Henson saw in Peary a successful young White American to whom he could attach his star to achieve his aspirations of becoming a recognized success in Black America.

By 1891 Henson had been selected to join Peary's first expeditionary team to explore the Arctic in pursuit of the North Pole. It is also remarkable for the time that Peary would present Henson in his first book, published in 1892, as essentially an equal to his four White assistants. From the very first expedition, Henson established himself as a valuable resource for Peary, and Peary counted on him for a number of tasks. Henson felt that Peary treated him quite fairly on that expedition. For example, Peary and his wife Josephine, the first known White female to travel to Northwest Greenland, celebrated the birthdays of each of their White assistants with a party. Henson often recounted with great pride his memory of his first birthday party, which was given by Mrs. Peary at their camp in Northwest Greenland on the occasion of his twenty-fourth birthday.

Peary and his team did not reach the North Pole in 1891, but they did explore much of Northern Greenland together. They were to make six additional attempts to reach the Pole from their Greenland base camps over the next seventeen years. So competitive were the efforts at the turn of the century by teams from many countries to reach the Pole that great excitement and often strife were generated between expeditions and among the explorers. Several conflicts developed on the early Peary expeditions, with some of Peary's assistants quitting on him in the field. Like most expedition leaders, Peary was known to be a fierce competitor and a driven man. Some of his White assistants, particularly those adventurers who sought fame and publicity in joining his expeditionary team, complained that Peary was simply demanding too much of them. But throughout all of this Henson remained with Peary, and indeed remained loyal to the goal of reaching the Pole, and rarely complained of the hardship. Josephine Peary once said of Henson that he was the only one of all of Peary's assistants to stick with her husband through all ordeals of his quest to discover the North Pole.

What I found particularly revealing in the documents, including diaries, that I uncovered in my research on Henson was that he lived in two different worlds, both literally and figuratively. When he was in the Arctic, he was treated by Peary and the Inuit "Eskimo" as an equal to the other White men on the expedition. In fact, after a few years of experience in Arctic culture and survival, Henson actually looked upon himself as technically superior to most of the White men whom Peary hired over the years to assist them in their North Pole expeditions. This is evident in some of the diaries in which the White men protested to Peary for his equal treatment of Henson, suggesting that Henson carried himself in such a way that he thought he too was a White man and equal to them. Henson often laughed off this kind of foolishness, for he knew that Peary's expedition could not survive without his skills.

From the very first expedition, some of Peary's assistants demonstrated the most blatant racism toward Henson. One of them, a Kentuckian named John Verhoeff, who had paid Peary to let him join the expedition, so resented Henson's presence (and that of Peary's wife, Josephine, whom he continually referred to in his diary as "the woman") that he verbally abused Henson and often referred to him by the oldest and most vile of American racial epithets. Much of his resentment against Henson had nothing to do with Henson's behavior toward him, but rather his jealousy of Henson's competence. For example, at one point in his diary Verhoeff protests strongly to Peary that, while he overslept, Henson had gone out to the sea and completed the tidal measurements that Peary had assigned to Verhoeff. Verhoeff also ridiculed Henson's efforts to learn the Inuit culture and language, skills which later served Henson and Peary well for Arctic survival and the attainment of the Pole. This tension between Verhoeff and Henson became so frequent and bitter that Mrs. Peary once ordered the two men outside the house to fight it out.

Curiously, Henson continued to try to win over his detractors. Often one finds a conciliatory remark in their diaries, suggesting that in spite of their mistreatment of Henson, he had been very helpful or done something rather nice for them. In Verhoeff's case, however, the abuse of Henson (and the Inuit "Eskimos") did not abate. It is still very curious that just days before his departure for the United States, Verhoeff "disappeared." Henson and the Inuit all said that they were certain he had fallen through the ice while out for a walk.

After each expedition between 1891 and 1908 Henson returned to America, which at the time was divided into two worlds, one Black and one White, revolving about each other like the planets, but almost never in more than superficial contact. In America he was no longer Peary's valued associate and equal; once he landed on American soil he was Peary's "colored assistant"—and, of course, Peary exploited this status. He could never join Peary and his fellow White elite in the elegant smoke-filled rooms of the National Geographic Society, and, although he lived in New York City, he was not permitted to become a member of the prestigious all-White male Explorers Club of which Peary was president. Henson spent his time between the expeditions working at the menial jobs that were available to a "colored" person at the time. The most available position for a Black man, and one that he took with some pride, was that of a porter on the trains that served as America's major mode of transportation at the time. While the position of porter was of low status in White American society, it served as a major source of employment and economic development in the African-American culture.

One of the most interesting and enjoyable posts Henson held, and one of the few that was arranged for him by Peary, was a position as assistant to the curator at the Museum of Natural History in New York, where he assisted in the preparation and display of the Arctic collection. By 1897 he had developed a thorough knowledge of the flora and fauna of Northwest Greenland, and assisted the curators in identifying and exhibiting specimens from Peary's collections.

Before one of his expeditions, Peary was asked by the well-known anthropologist Franz Boas to bring back to the United States some Inuit who could be presented to the public as part of the Museum's live exhibitions or collections. This was at the time a common practice of some European and Euro-American institutions. In some European countries such as Germany and in the United States certain zoos exhibited captive Africans just as they did animals. Although Boas had complained about the prejudice he had experienced in his efforts to be treated as "white," he saw no contradiction in treating the Inuit people as animals to be exploited and exhibited in "collections." Peary, on the other hand, sought credibility as a scientist, and from his first expedition had always taken some "natural scientist" with him. In 1891, for example, Peary brought along an ornithologist to collect and classify the birds (and other fauna) in the Arctic Highland, as Northwest Greenland was called at that time. He also took along a young physician as an assistant named Frederick A. Cook (later to become his nemesis) whom he assigned to studying the physical characteristics of the Inuit men and women, living and dead. At one point during the 1891 expedition Cook was threatened by the native Inuit for disturbing their family's gravesites and collecting the skeletons to be shipped to America. In fact, the threat to Peary's visiting expedition was so serious that Henson, to whom Peary had entrusted the protection of Mrs. Peary, had to take her some miles away from the campsite and hide her in a cave until the conflict had subsided. Some years ago I found many of the skeletal remains collected by Peary and Dr. Cook in 1891, stored away in a museum at Harvard University. It was only after careful examination of the skull of one of these Polar Inuit skeletons that I found a tiny white heavy paper tag, hidden in the back of an eye socket, on which was written the name of the collector, "Lieutenant Robert E. Peary."

It was apparently Peary's desire to be considered a scientist or substantial contributor to the field of anthropology that made him bring back to America five Inuit adults and one six-year-old boy named Mene for exhibition at the Museum of Natural History. According to the Inuit, Henson had strong reservations about taking the Inuit from their Polar homeland to the United States. After several money-making exhibitions of the Eskimos in full native garb aboard Peary's ship, and later in the Museum of Natural History, the Inuit began to take ill. Their health rapidly deteriorated from exposure to new microbes, and they were hospitalized in New York. Matthew Henson was the only man in New York or perhaps in the entire United States who was known to speak the Inuit language fluently. He was summoned by the museum's curator and Peary to translate for the sick Inuit and their doctors. It was Matthew Henson who attended the Inuit as they lay dying from infectious respiratory diseases. It was he who promised to take word back to their families about their experiences and their deaths. He also promised to help their families survive in their absence by providing for them hunting apparatus and other items. Only two of the Inuit survived their stay in the United States: the six-year-old Mene and one older man. Mene was adopted by an American who was associated with the museum, and the surviving adult returned to his home in Northwest Greenland.

The tragic end to this story was that instead of burying the remains of the Inuit or sending them back to Greenland on one of Peary's voyages, the skeletons were defleshed and mounted for exhibition in the Museum of Natural History. Mene, who was told that his father had been buried, later discovered to his shock that one of the articulated skeletons he had observed in a display case in the Museum of Natural History was that of his father. Being from a society in which human skeletal remains are sacred, even the six-year-old knew that this was a desecration of his father's remains.

Some years later Henson helped Mene return to Greenland, and subsequently provided him with enough hunting equipment and supplies to enable him to support himself in a homeland he had left as a small child. Although he tried for some years to adjust, it was extraordinarily difficult for Mene to adapt to conditions in Greenland, and he eventually returned to America and wandered about seeking menial jobs until he died as a young man of apparent respiratory illness while working in New Hampshire.

In 1909 Peary was credited with discovering the North Pole. The claim was not immediately believed by all, because Peary's former assistant, Dr. Frederick Cook, had himself set out on an expedition to reach the North Pole a year earlier, and claimed to have reached the Pole before Peary. Although Cook was later shown to be a monumental fraud, he nevertheless did a great deal of harm to Peary's credibility as the discoverer of the North Pole. Of course, if Peary could be shown not to have reached the Pole, it means that Henson did not make it either. It is interesting that Henson did not publicly join the fray. This was probably for two reasons: first, Peary forbade Henson's involvement in the controversy, thinking that it would continually raise the race question; and second, Henson was reluctant to condemn Cook publicly (although in private he ridiculed the idea that Cook could travel more than a few miles on his own in the Arctic, let alone to the North Pole) because following the expedition in 1891 Henson had developed a severe case of snow blindness, and it was Dr. Cook who treated him and let him spend his convalescence in Cook's mother's home (also an atypical interracial gesture for that era). In the ensuing Polar discovery controversy, Henson and the Inuit were essentially left out of the equation because they were not considered by the Whites of that era to be "credible witnesses." The notorious racist Adolphus Greeley, of the U.S. Navy, who had some years earlier lost his entire crew on an Arctic expedition and had survived with a few of his men only by eating the others, publicly stated that he did not believe Peary had reached the Pole, because all he had to prove it was "an ignorant Negro." Peary had earlier criticized Greeley for failing to save his men because he callously ignored the Eskimo survival traditions as racially inferior.

In my research on Henson I chose to go directly to those "noncredible" witnesses of color for information about the

Polar expeditions. Many of their descriptions of the Polar expeditions undertaken by both Peary and Cook have been thoroughly documented by the distinguished Danish explorer Peter Freuchen, who for many years lived among the Polar Inuit, and married an Inuit woman. Freuchen, who was elected to membership in the Explorers Club, repeated on many occasions the accounts of the Inuit who traveled to the North Pole with Peary and Henson. He cited their evidence of distance and speed of travel as proof that Peary, Henson, Ootah, Seegloo, Oqueah, and Egingwah all stood at 90° North on April 6, 1909. In contrast, the two Inuit men who traveled with Cook a year earlier told Freuchen that they did not know whether they had reached the Pole or not, they only knew that Cook took them to some distant part of Ellesmere Island, where they lived in a cave for several months and hunted for food, and could always see a mountain in the background. Of course, there are no mountains at the geographic North Pole.

Perhaps the most intriguing person that I uncovered in my research was a man of mixed-race background whose father was a Dane and mother an indigenous Inuit. Dr. Knut Rasmussen had earned a doctoral degree in Copenhagen, in a field similar to anthropological studies. Because of his mixed-race background, he too was not considered a "credible witness" among the White elite of America, and has been totally overlooked by most White researchers who have for nearly a century written about the North Pole discovery. Rasmussen said that the moment he talked with the Inuit that had accompanied Cook on his so-called North Pole journey and viewed Cook's records, he "knew it was a scandal." Yet his view was never taken seriously and still today some wish to credit Cook with the North Pole discovery. It cannot be overlooked that much of the recent controversy about who discovered the North Pole still invokes the concept of the White "credible witness." Some of the most recent accounts of the North Pole discovery are only thinly veiled attempts to discredit Peary (and thus Henson) and exalt the fraudulent Cook.

It was unknown to the American public and most of the world that during the course of the expeditions Peary and Henson had essentially acquired wives in the Arctic. While some explorers and sailors who traveled to Northwest Greenland were able to conjecture that certain members of the Peary Polar expedition had fathered children with Inuit women in Greenland, this had never been demonstrated conclusively. In 1986 I traveled to the northernmost settlements in the world in Northwest Greenland, where I interviewed numerous Inuit who are the descendants of Ootah, Seegloo, Oqueah, and Egingwah—the four Inuit who accompanied Peary and Henson to the Pole. The stories they had to tell were nothing short of fascinating. But perhaps the most important thing I learned was that the admiration the Inuit of the late 1800s had for the man they called Mahripaluq (meaning "Matt, the kind one") lives on today in Northwest Greenland. As Ootah once said, they still sing of him in their songs and talk of him in their stories. It was these Inuit men and women who told me of the "descendants of the expedition." I was directed to the village of Moriussaq, where I was greeted by the Inuit with a humorous fascination, almost as if they were expecting me. I later learned it was my dark skin that made them believe I was a Henson who had come to Greenland to find his relatives. The climax of my arrival in Moriussaq was when another dark-skinned man with curly hair came out to greet me and said, "I am Mahripaluq's son."

Henson was a single man when he met Akatingwah and later fathered a son with her in 1906. The son was named

Anaukaq, and his only contacts with his father were during the period of the expeditions between 1906 and 1909. His mother later married an Inuit man named Kitdlaq who adopted him and raised him in the Inuit "Eskimo" tradition.

Peary, a married father of two in the United States, had a virtual wife in Greenland, the Inuit woman Alakaceena, whom he had known and been attracted to since she was sixteen years old. He fathered two sons with Alakaceena, one who lived to the age of twenty-seven and died of what the Inuit call "a hole in the stomach," and another who died aged ninety-two in 1998. I met Peary's son Kali (pronounced *Kahree* by most of the Inuit) during that same 1986 visit. After getting to know both men and extensive interviews, they both indicated how much they had always wished to visit the land of their fathers, and, as Anaukaq put it, to "touch a relative." While I could not promise them that I could help them to achieve their lifelong aim, I did promise that I would try. After extensive planning and a letter-writing campaign to officials in both the United States and Denmark, I was finally able to secure permission for the Inuit sons of Henson and Peary to visit the United States. Over a two-week period in 1987 I had the good fortune to take Anaukaq, Kali, and ten of their respective offspring on a tour of many sites of significance in their fathers' lives, to enable them to lay wreaths at their respective fathers' gravesites, and for the first time in their lives to meet their American relatives.

It was during this visit of Henson's and Peary's surviving sons and grandchildren that I came to focus on the disparity of the two explorers' fates in life and in death. To the surprise of the visiting Inuit, Peary was commemorated by a large granite monument in Arlington National Cemetery that deemed him "The Discoverer of the North Pole," while

Henson, whom the Inuit admired the most, was buried in a common grave in Woodlawn Cemetery in New York City. While sitting with Anaukaq at his father's gravesite, I promised to do everything in my power to have Henson reinterred in Arlington National Cemetery with full ceremonial honors. Again, I had no idea how I would fulfill this ambitious undertaking.

In 1987 I petitioned the president of the United States for permission to reinter Matthew Henson with honors in Arlington National Cemetery. After a year of making the case for Matthew Henson's place in history, my request was granted, and on April 6, 1988, on the seventy-ninth anniversary of the discovery of the Pole, Matthew Alexander Henson was reinterred next to Peary at Arlington National Cemetery with full honors. He would have been proud.

S. ALLEN COUNTER, D.M.Sc., Ph.D.
Neuroscience professor at Harvard Medical School and Director of the Harvard Foundation

FOREWORD

FRIENDS OF ARCTIC EXPLORATION and discovery, with whom I have come in contact, and many whom I know only by letter, have been greatly interested in the fact of a colored man being an effective member of a serious Arctic expedition, and going north, not once, but numerous times during a period of over twenty years, in a way that showed that he not only could and did endure all the stress of Arctic conditions and work, but that he evidently found pleasure in the work.

The example and experience of Matthew Henson, who has been a member of each and of all my Arctic expeditions, since '91 (my trip in 1886 was taken before I knew Henson) is only another one of the multiplying illustrations of the fact that race, or color, or bringing-up, or environment, count nothing against a determined heart, if it is backed and aided by intelligence.

Henson proved his fitness by long and thorough apprenticeship, and his participation in the final victory which planted the Stars and Stripes at the North Pole, and won for this country the international prize of nearly four centuries, is a distinct credit and feather in the cap of his race.

As I wired Charles W. Anderson, collector of internal revenue, and chairman of the dinner which was given to Henson in New York, in October 1909, on the occasion of the presentation to him of a gold watch and chain by his admirers:

> I congratulate you and your race upon Matthew Henson. He has driven home to the world your great adaptability and the fiber of which you are made. He has added to the moral stature of every intelligent man among you. His is the hard-earned reward of tried loyalty, persistence, and endurance. He should be an everlasting example to your young men that these qualities will win whatever object they are directed at. He deserves every attention you can show him. I regret that it is impossible for me to be present at your dinner. My compliments to your assembled guests.

It would be superfluous to enlarge on Henson in this introduction. His work in the north has already spoken for itself and for him. His book will speak for itself and him.

Yet two of the interesting points which present themselves in connection with his work may be noted.

Henson, son of the tropics, has proven through years, his ability to stand tropical, temperate, and the fiercest stress of frigid, climate and exposure, while on the other hand, it is well known that the inhabitants of the highest north, tough and hardy as they are to the rigors of their own climate, succumb very quickly to the vagaries of even a temperate climate. The question presents itself at once: "Is it a difference in physical fiber, or in brain and willpower, or is the difference in the climatic conditions themselves?"

Again it is an interesting fact that in the final conquest of the "prize of the centuries," not alone individuals, but *races* were represented. On that bitter brilliant day in April 1909, when the Stars and Stripes floated at the North Pole, Caucasian, Ethiopian, and Mongolian stood side by side at the apex of the earth, in the harmonious companionship resulting from hard work, exposure, danger, and a common object.

R. E. PEARY
Washington, Dec. 1911

INTRODUCTION

ONE OF THE FIRST QUESTIONS which Commander Peary was asked when he returned home from his long, patient, and finally successful struggle to reach the Pole was how it came about that, beside the four Esquimos, Matt Henson, a Negro, was the only man to whom was accorded the honor of accompanying him on the final dash to the goal.

The question was suggested no doubt by the thought that it was but natural that the positions of greatest responsibility and honor on such an expedition would as a matter of course fall to the white men of the party rather than to a Negro. To this question, however, Commander Peary replied, in substance:

> Matthew A. Henson, my Negro assistant, has been with me in one capacity or another since my second trip to Nicaragua in 1887. I have taken him on each and all of my expeditions, except the first, and also without exception on each of my farthest sledge trips. This position I have given him primarily because of

> his adaptability and fitness for the work and secondly on account of his loyalty. He is a better dog driver and can handle a sledge better than any man living, except some of the best Esquimo hunters themselves.

In short, Matthew Henson, next to Commander Peary, held and still holds the place of honor in the history of the expedition that finally located the position of the Pole, because he was the best man for the place. During twenty-three years of faithful service he had made himself indispensable. From the position of a servant he rose to that of companion and assistant in one of the most dangerous and difficult tasks that was ever undertaken by men. In extremity, when both the danger and the difficulty were greatest, the Commander wanted by his side the man upon whose skill and loyalty he could put the most absolute dependence and when that man turned out to be black instead of white, the Commander was not only willing to accept the service but was at the same time generous enough to acknowledge it.

There never seems to have been any doubt in Commander Peary's mind about Henson's part and place in the expedition.

Matt Henson, who was born in Charles County, Maryland, August 8, 1866, began life as a cabin-boy on an ocean steamship, and before he met Commander Peary had already made a voyage to China. He was eighteen years old when he made the acquaintance of Commander Peary which gave him his chance. During the twenty-three years in which he was the companion of the explorer he not only had time and opportunity to perfect himself in his knowledge of the books, but he acquired a good practical knowledge of everything that was a necessary part of the daily life in the ice-bound wilderness of polar exploration. He was at times a blacksmith, a carpenter, and a cook. He was thoroughly acquainted with the life, customs, and language of the Esquimos. He himself built the sledges with which the journey to the Pole was successfully completed. He could not merely drive a dog-team or skin a musk-ox with the skill of a native, but he was something of a navigator as well. In this way Mr. Henson made himself not only the most trusted but the most useful member of the expedition.

I am reminded in this connection that Matthew Henson is not the first colored man who by his fidelity and devotion has made himself the trusty companion of the men who have explored and opened up the western continent. Even in the days when the Negro had little or no opportunity to show his ability as a leader, he proved himself at least a splendid follower, and there are few great adventures in which the American white man has engaged where he has not been accompanied by a colored man.

Nearly all the early Spanish explorers were accompanied by Negroes. It is said that the first ship built in America was constructed by the slaves of Vasquez de Ayllon, who attempted to establish a Spanish settlement where Jamestown, Virginia, was later founded. Balboa had 30 Negroes with him, and they assisted him in constructing the first ship on the Pacific coast. Three hundred slaves were brought to this country by Cortez, the conqueror of Mexico, and it is said that the town of Santiago del Principe was founded by Negro slaves who later rebelled against their Spanish masters.

Of the story of those earlier Negro explorers we have, aside from the Negro Estevan or "little Steve," who was the guide and leader in the search for the fabulous seven cities, almost nothing more than a passing reference in the accounts which have come down to us. Now, a race which has come up from slavery; which is just now for the first time learning to build for itself homes, churches, schools;

which is learning for the first time to start banks, organize insurance companies, erect manufacturing plants, establish hospitals; a race which is doing all the fundamental things for the first time; which has, in short, its history before it instead of behind; such a race in such conditions needs for its own encouragement, as well as to justify the hopes of its friends, the records of the members of the race who have been a part of any great and historic achievement.

For this reason, as well as for others; for the sake of my race as well as the truth of history; I am proud and glad to welcome this account of his adventure from a man who has not only honored the race of which he is a member, but has proven again that courage, fidelity, and ability are honored and rewarded under a black skin as well as under a white.

BOOKER T. WASHINGTON
Principal, Tuskegee Normal
and Industrial Institute

A NEGRO EXPLORER AT THE NORTH POLE

CHAPTER I

The Early Years: Schoolboy, Cabin-Boy, Seaman, and Lieutenant Peary's Body-Servant—First Trips to the Arctic

WHEN THE NEWS OF THE DISCOVERY of the North Pole, by Commander Peary, was first sent to the world, a distinguished citizen of New York City, well versed in the affairs of the Peary Arctic Club, made the statement that he was sure that Matt Henson had been with Commander Peary on the day of the discovery. There were not many people who knew who Henson was, or the reason why the gentleman had made the remark, and, when asked why he was so certain, he explained that, for the best part of the twenty years of Commander Peary's Arctic work, his faithful and often only companion was Matthew Alexander Henson.

To-day there is a more general knowledge of Commander Peary, his work and his success, and a vague understanding of the fact that Commander Peary's sole companion from the realm of civilization, when he stood at the North Pole, was Matthew A. Henson, a Colored Man.

To satisfy the demand of perfectly natural curiosity, I have undertaken to write a brief autobiography, giving particularly an account of my Arctic work.

I was born in Charles County, Maryland, August 8, 1866. The place of my birth was on the Potomac River, about forty-four miles below Washington, D.C. Slavery days were over forever when I was born. Besides, my parents were both free born before me, and in my mother's veins ran some white blood. At an early age, my parents were induced to leave the country and remove to Washington, D.C. My mother died when I was seven years old. I was taken in charge by my uncle, who sent me to school, the "N Street School" in Washington, D.C., which I attended for over six years. After leaving school I went to Baltimore, Md., where I shipped as cabin-boy, on board a vessel bound for China. After my first voyage I became an able-bodied seaman, and for four years followed the sea in that capacity, sailing to China, Japan, Manilla, North Africa, Spain, France, and through the Black Sea to Southern Russia.

It was while I was in Washington, D.C., in 1888, that I first attracted the attention of Commander Peary, who at that time was a civil engineer in the United States Navy, with the rank of lieutenant, and it was with the instinct of my race that I recognized in him the qualities that made me willing to engage myself in his service. I accompanied him as his body-servant to Nicaragua. I was his messenger at the League Island Navy Yard, and from the beginning of his second expedition to the Arctic regions, in 1891, I have been a member of every expedition of his, in the capacity of assistant: a term that covers a multitude of duties, abilities, and responsibilities.

The narrative that follows is a record of the last and successful expedition of the Peary Arctic Club, which had as its attainment the discovery of the North Pole, and is compiled from notes made by me at different times during the course of the expedition. I did endeavor to keep a diary or journal of daily events during my last trip, and did not find it difficult aboard the ship while sailing north, or when in winter-quarters at Cape Sheridan, but I found it impossible to make daily entries while in the field, on account of the constant necessity of concentrating my attention on the real business of the expedition. Entries were made daily of the records of temperature and the estimates of distance traveled; and when solar observations were made the results were always carefully noted. There were opportunities to complete the brief entries on several occasions while out on the ice, notably the six days' enforced delay at the "Big Lead," 84° north, the twelve hours preceding the return of Captain Bartlett at 87° 47′ north, and the thirty-three hours at North Pole, while Commander Peary was determining to a certainty his position. During the return from the Pole to Cape Columbia, we were so urged by the knowledge of the supreme necessity of speed that the thought of recording the events of that part of the journey did not occur to me so forcibly as to compel me to pay heed to it, and that story was written aboard the ship while waiting for favorable conditions to sail toward home lands.

It was in June, 1891, that I started on my first trip to the Arctic regions, as a member of what was known as the "North Greenland Expedition." Mrs. Peary accompanied her husband, and among the members of the expedition were Dr. Frederick A. Cook, of Brooklyn, N.Y., Mr. Langdon Gibson, of Flushing, N.Y., and Mr. Eivind Astrüp, of Christiania, Norway, who had the honor of being the companion of Commander Peary in the first crossing of North Greenland—and of having an Esquimo at Cape York become so fond of him that he named his son for him! It was on this voyage north that Peary's leg was broken.

Mr. John M. Verhoeff, a stalwart young Kentuckian, was also an enthusiastic member of the party. When the expedition was ready to sail home the following summer, he lost his life by falling in a crevasse in a glacier. His body was never recovered. On the first and the last of Peary's expeditions, success was marred by tragedy. On the last expedition, Professor Ross G. Marvin, of Cornell University, lost his life by being drowned in the Arctic Ocean, on his return from his farthest north, a farther north than had ever been made by any other explorers except the members of the last expedition. Both Verhoeff and Marvin were good friends of mine, and I respect and venerate their memories.

Naturally, the impressions formed on my first visit to the Land of Ice and Snow were the most lasting, but in the coming years I was to learn more and more that such a life was no picnic, and to realize what primitive life meant. I was to live with a people who, the scientists stated, represented the earliest form of human life, living in what is known as the Stone Age, and I was to revert to that stage of life by leaps and bounds, and to emerge from it by the same sudden means. Many and many a time, for periods covering more than twelve months, I have been to all intents an Esquimo, with Esquimos for companions, speaking their language, dressing in the same kind of clothes, living in the same kind of dens, eating the same food, enjoying their pleasures, and frequently sharing their griefs. I have come to love these people. I know every man, woman, and child in their tribe. They are my friends and they regard me as theirs.

After the first return to civilization, I was to come back to the savage, ice- and rock-bound country seven times more. It was in June 1893, that I again sailed north with Commander Peary and his party on board the *Falcon,* a larger ship than the *Kite,* the one we sailed north in on the previous expedition, and with a much larger equipment, including several burros from Colorado, which were intended for ice-cap work, but which did not make good, making better dog-food instead. Indeed the dogs made life a burden for the poor brutes from the very start. Mrs. Peary was again a member of the expedition, as well as another woman, Mrs. Cross, who acted as Mrs. Peary's maid and nurse. It was on this trip that I adopted the orphan Esquimo boy, Kudlooktoo, his mother having died just previous to our arrival at the Red Cliffs. After this boy was washed and scrubbed by me, his long hair cut short, and his greasy, dirty clothes of skins and furs burned, a new suit made of odds and ends collected from different wardrobes on the ship made him a presentable Young American. I was proud of him, and he of me. He learned to speak English and slept underneath my bunk.

This expedition was larger in numbers than the previous one, but the results, owing to the impossible weather conditions, were by no means successful, and the following season all of the expedition returned to the United States except Commander Peary, Hugh J. Lee, and myself. When the expedition returned, there were two who went back who had not come north with us. Miss Marie Ahnighito Peary, aged about ten months, who first saw the light of day at Anniversary Lodge on the 12th of the previous September, was taken by her mother to her kinfolks in the South. Mrs. Peary also took a young Esquimo girl, well known among us as "Miss Bill," along with her, and kept her for nearly a year, when she gladly permitted her to return to

Greenland and her own people. Miss Bill is now grown up, and has been married three times and widowed, not by death but by desertion. She is known as a "Holy Terror." I do not know the reason why, but I have my suspicions.

The memory of the winter of 1894 and 1895 and the summer following will never leave me. The events of the journey to 87° 6′ in 1906 and the discovery of the North Pole in 1909 are indelibly impressed on my mind, but the recollections of the long race with death across the 450 miles of the ice-cap of North Greenland in 1895, with Commander Peary and Hugh Lee, are still the most vivid.

For weeks and weeks, across the seemingly never-ending wastes of the ice-cap of North Greenland, I marched with Peary and Lee from Independence Bay and the land beyond back to Anniversary Lodge. We started on April 1, 1895, with three sledges and thirty-seven dogs, with the object of determining to a certainty the northeastern terminus of Greenland. We reached the northern land beyond the ice-cap, but the condition of the country did not allow much exploration, and after killing a few musk-oxen we started on June 1 to make our return. We had one sledge and nine dogs.

We reached Anniversary Lodge on June 25, with one dog.

The Grim Destroyer had been our constant companion, and it was months before I fully recovered from the effects of that struggle. When I left for home and God's Country the following September, on board the good old *Kite,* it was with the strongest resolution to never again! no more! forever! leave my happy home in warmer lands.

NEVERTHELESS, the following summer I was again "Northward Bound," with Commander Peary, to help him secure, and bring to New York, the three big meteorites that he and Lee had discovered during the winter of 1894–1895.

The meteorites known as "The Woman" and "The Dog" were secured with comparative ease, and the work of getting the large seventy-ton meteor, known as "The Tent," into such a position as to insure our securing it the following summer, was done, so it was not strange that the following summer I was again in Greenland, but the meteorite was not brought away that season.

It is well known that the chief characteristic of Commander Peary is persistency which, coupled with fortitude, is the secret of his success. The next summer, 1897, he was again at the island after his prize, and he got it this time and brought it safely to New York, where it now reposes in the "American Museum of Natural History." As usual I was a member of the party, and my back still aches when I think of the hard work I did to help load that monster aboard the *Hope.*

It was during that voyage that Commander Peary announced his determination to discover the North Pole, and the following years (from 1898 to 1902) were spent in the Arctic.

In 1900, the American record of Farthest North, held by Lockwood and Brainard, was equaled and exceeded; their cairn visited and their records removed. On April 21, 1902, a new American record of 84° 17′ was made by Commander Peary, further progress north being frustrated by a lack of provisions and by a lane of open water, more than a mile wide. This lead or lane of open water I have since become more familiarly acquainted with. We have called it many names, but it is popularly known as the "Big Lead." Going north, meeting it can be depended upon. It is situated just a few miles north of the 84th parallel, and is believed to mark the continental shelf of the land masses in the Northern Hemisphere.

During the four years from 1898 to 1902, which were continuously spent in the regions about North Greenland, we had every experience, except death, that had ever fallen to the lot of the explorers who had preceded us, and more than once we looked death squarely in the face. Besides, we had many experiences that earlier explorers did not meet. In January 1899, Commander Peary froze his feet so badly that all but one of his toes fell off.

After the return home, in 1902, it was three years before Commander Peary made another attack on the Pole, but during those years he was not resting.

He was preparing to launch his final and "sincerely to be hoped" successful expedition, and in July 1905, in the newly built ship, *Roosevelt,* we were again "Poleward-bound." The following September, the *Roosevelt* reached Cape Sheridan, latitude 82° 27′ north, under her own steam, a record unequaled by any other vessel, sail or steam.

Early the next year, the negotiation of the Arctic Ocean was commenced, not as oceans usually are negotiated, but as this ocean must be, by men, sledges, and dogs. The field party consisted of twenty-six men, twenty sledges, and one hundred and thirty dogs.

That was an open winter and an early spring, very desirable conditions in some parts of the world, but very undesirable to us on the northern coast of Greenland. The ice-pack began disintegrating much too early that year to suit, but we pushed on, and had it not been for furious storms enforcing delays and losses of many precious days, the Pole would have been reached. As it was, Commander Peary and his party got to 87° 6′ north, thereby breaking *all records,* and in spite of incredible hardships, hunger, and cold, returned safely with all of the expedition, and on Christmas Eve the *Roosevelt,* after a most trying voyage, entered New York Harbor, somewhat battered but still seaworthy.

Despite the fact that it was to be his last attempt, Commander Peary no sooner reached home than he announced his intention to return, this time to be the last, and this time to win.

However, a year intervened, and it was not until July 6, 1908, with the God-Speed and good wishes of President Roosevelt, that the good ship named in his honor set sail again. The narrative of that voyage, and the story of the discovery of the North Pole, follow.

The ages of the wild, misgiving mystery of the North Pole are over, to-day, and forever it stands under the folds of Old Glory.

CHAPTER II

Off for the Pole—How the Other Explorers Looked—The Lamb-Like Esquimos—Arrival at Etah

JULY 6, 1908: We're off! For a year and a half I have waited for this order, and now we have cast off. The shouting and the tumult ceases, the din of whistles, bells, and throats dies out, and once again the long, slow surge of the ocean hits the good ship that we have embarked in. It was at one-thirty P.M. to-day that I saw the last hawse-line cast adrift, and felt the throb of the engines of our own ship. Chief Wardwell is on the job, and from now on it is due north.

Oyster Bay, Long Island Sound: We are expecting President Roosevelt. The ship has been named in his honor and has already made one voyage towards the North Pole, farther north than any ship has ever made.

July 7: At anchor, the soft wooded hills of Long Island give me a curious impression. I am waiting for the command to attack the savage ice- and rock-bound fortress of the North, and here instead we are at anchor in the neighborhood of sheep grazing in green fields.

Sydney, C.B., July 17, 1908: All of the expedition are aboard and those going home have gone. Mrs. Peary and the children, Mr. Borup's father, and Mr. Harry Whitney, and some other guests were the last to leave the *Roosevelt,* and have given us a last good-by from the tug, which came alongside to take them off.

Good-by all. Every one is sending back a word to some one he has left behind, but I have said my good-bys a long time ago, and as I waved my hand in parting salutation to the little group on the deck of the tug, my thoughts were with my wife, and I hoped when she next heard of me it would be with feelings of joy and happiness, and that she would be glad she had permitted me to leave her for an absence that might never end.

The tenderfeet, as the Commander calls them, are the Doctor, Professor MacMillan, and young Mr. Borup. The Doctor is a fine-looking, big fellow, John W. Goodsell, and has a swarthy complexion and straight hair; on meeting me he told me that he was well acquainted with me by reputation, and hoped to know me more intimately.

Professor Donald B. MacMillan is a professor in a college in Massachusetts, near Worcester, and I am going to cultivate his acquaintance.

Mr. George Borup is the kid, only twenty-one years old but well set up for his age, always ready to laugh, and has thick, curly hair. I understand he is a record-breaker in athletics. He will need his athletic ability on this trip. I am making no judgments or comments on these fellows now. Wait; I have seen too many enthusiastic starters, and I am sorry to say some of them did not finish well.

All of the rest of the members of the expedition are the same as were on the first trip of the *Roosevelt:*—Commander Peary, Captain Bartlett, Professor Marvin, Chief Engineer Wardwell, Charley Percy the steward, and myself. The crew has been selected by Captain Bartlett, and are mostly strangers to me.

Commander Peary is too well known for me to describe him at length; thick reddish hair turning gray; heavy, bushy eyebrows shading his "sharpshooter's eyes" of steel gray, and long mustache. His hair grows rapidly and, when on the march, a thick heavy beard quickly appears. He is six feet tall, very graceful, and well built, especially about the chest and shoulders; long arms, and legs slightly bowed. Since losing his toes, he walks with a peculiar slide-like stride. He has a voice clear and loud, and words never fail him.

Captain Bartlett is about my height and weight. He has short, curly, light-brown hair and red cheeks; is slightly round-shouldered, due to the large shoulder-muscles caused by pulling the oars, and is as quick in his actions as a cat. His manner and conduct indicate that he has always been the leader of his crowd from boyhood up, and there is no man on this ship that he would be afraid to tackle. He is a young man (thirty-three years old) for a ship captain, but he knows his job.

Professor Marvin is a quiet, earnest person, and has had plenty of practical experience besides his splendid education. He is rapidly growing bald; his face is rather thin, and his neck is long. He has taken great interest in me and, being a teacher, has tried to teach me. Although I hope to perfect myself in navigation, my knowledge so far consists only of knot and splice seamanship, and I need to master the mathematical end.

The Chief Engineer, Mr. Wardwell, is a fine-looking, ruddy-complexioned giant, with the most honest eyes I have ever looked into. His hair is thinning and is almost pure white, and I should judge him to be about forty-five years old. He has the greatest patience, and I have never seen him lose his temper or get rattled.

Charley Percy is Commander Peary's oldest hand, next to me. He is our steward, and sees to it that we are properly fed while aboard ship, and he certainly does see to it with credit to himself.

From Sydney to Hawks Harbor, where we met the *Erik,* has been uneventful except for the odor of the *Erik,* which is loaded with whale-meat and can be smelled for miles. We passed St. Paul's Island and Cape St. George early in the day and through the Straits of Belle Isle to Hawks Harbor, where there is a whale-factory. From here we leave for Turnavik.

We have been racing with the *Erik* all day, and have beaten her to this place. Captain Bartlett's father owns it, and we loaded a lot of boots and skins, which the Captain's father had ready for us. From here we sail to the Esquimo country of North Greenland, without a stop if possible, as the Commander has no intention of visiting any of the Danish settlements in South Greenland.

Cape York is our next point, and the ship is sailing free. Aside from the excitement of the start, and the honor of receiving the personal visit of the President, and his words of encouragement and cheer, the trip so far has been uneventful; and I have busied myself in putting my cabin in order, and making myself useful in overhauling and stowing provisions in the afterhold.

July 24: Still northward-bound, with the sea rolling and washing over the ship; and the *Erik* in the distance seems to be getting her share of the wash. She is loaded heavily with fresh whale-meat, and is purposely keeping in leeward of us to spare us the discomfort of the odor.

July 25 and 26: Busy with my carpenter's kit in the Commander's cabin and elsewhere. There has been heavy rain and seas, and we have dropped the *Erik* completely. The *Roosevelt* is going fine. We can see the Greenland coast plainly and to-day, the 29th, we raised and passed Disco Island. Icebergs on all sides. The light at midnight is almost as bright as early evening twilight in New York on the Fourth of July and the ice-blink of the interior ice-cap is quite plain. We have gone through Baffin's Bay with a rush and raised Duck Island about ten A.M. and passed and dropped it by two P.M.

I was ashore on Duck Island in 1891, on my first voyage north, and I remember distinctly the cairn the party built and the money they deposited in it. I wonder if it is still there? There is little use for money up here, and the place is seldom visited except by men from the whalers, when their ships are locked in by ice.

From here it is two hundred miles due north to Cape York.

August 1: Arrived at Cape York Bay and went ashore with the party to communicate with the Esquimos of whom there were three families. They remembered us and were dancing up and down the shore, and waving to us in welcome, and as soon as the bow of the boat had grazed the little beach, willing hands helped to run her up on shore. These people are hospitable and helpful, and always willing, sometimes too willing. As an example, I will tell how, at a settlement farther north, we were going ashore in one of the whale-boats. Captain Bartlett was forward, astraddle of the bow with the boat-hook in his hands to fend off the blocks of ice, and knew perfectly well where he wanted to land, but the group of excited Esquimos were in his way and though he ordered them back, they continued running about and getting in his way. In a very short while the

Captain lost patience and commenced to talk loudly and with excitement; immediately Sipsoo took up his language and parrot-like started to repeat the Captain's exact words: "Get back there, get back—how in —— do you expect me to make a landing?" And thus does the innocent lamb of the North acquire a civilized tongue.

It is amusing to hear Kudlooktoo in the most charming manner give Charley a cussing that from any one else would cause Charley to break his head open.

For the last week I have been busy, with "Matt! The Commander wants you," "Matt do this," and "Matt do that," and with going ashore and trading for skins, dogs, lines, and other things; and also walrus-hunting. I have been up to my neck in work, and have had small opportunity to keep my diary up to date. We have all put on heavy clothing; not the regular fur clothes for the winter, but our thickest civilized clothing, that we would wear in midwinter in the States. In the middle of the day, if the sun shines, the heat is felt; but if foggy or cloudy, the heavy clothing is comfortable.

All of the Esquimos want to come aboard and stay aboard. Some we want and will take along, but there are others we will not have or take along on a bet, and the pleasant duty of telling them so and putting them ashore falls to me. It is not a pleasant job to disappoint these people, but they would be a burden to us and in our way. Besides, we have left them a plentiful supply of needfuls, and our trading with them has been fair and generous.

The "Crow's-Nest" has been rigged upon the mainmast, and this morning, after breakfast, Mr. Whitney, three Esquimos, and myself started in Mr. Whitney's motor-boat to hunt walrus. The motor gave out very shortly after the start, and the oars had to be used. We were fortunate in getting two walrus, which I shot, and then we returned to the ship for the whale-boat. We left the ship with three more Esquimos in the whale-boat, and got four more walrus.

Sunday, at Kangerdlooksoah; the land of the reindeer, and the one pleasant appearing spot on this coast. Mr. Whitney and his six Esquimo guides have gone hunting for deer, and I have been ashore to trade for dogs and furs, and have gotten twenty-seven dogs, sealskin-lines for lashings, a big bearskin, and some foxskins. I try to get furskins from animals that were killed when in full fur and before they have started to shed, but some of the skins I have traded in are raw, and will have to be dried.

I have had the disagreeable job of putting the undesirable ashore, and it was like handling a lot of sulky school children.

Seegloo, the dog-owner, is invited to bring his pack aboard and is easily persuaded. He will get a Springfield rifle and loading-outfit and also a Winchester, if he will sell, and he is more than willing.

And this is the story of day after day from Cape York to Etah Harbor, which we reached on August 12.

CHAPTER III

Finding of Rudolph Franke—Whitney Landed—
Trading and Coaling—Fighting the Ice-Packs

AT ETAH WE TAKE ON THE FINAL load of coal from the *Erik* and the other supplies she has for us, and from now on it will be farewell to all the world; we will be alone with our company, and our efforts will be towards the north and our evasive goal.

At Etah, on going ashore, we were met by the most hopelessly dirty, unkempt, filth-littered human being any of us had ever seen, or could ever have imagined; a white man with long matted hair and beard, who could speak very little English and that only between cries, whimperings, and whines, and whose legs were swollen out of all shape from the scurvy. He was Rudolph Franke and had been left here the year before by Dr. F. A. Cook, an old acquaintance of mine, who had been a member of other expeditions of the Commander's.

Franke was in a bad way, and the burden of his wail was, "Take me away from this, I have permission, see, here is Dr.

Cook's letter," and he showed a letter from Dr. Cook, authorizing him to leave, if opportunity offered. Dr. Goodsell looked him over and pronounced him unfit to remain in the Arctic any longer than it would take a ship to get him out, and the Commander had him kindly treated, cleaned, medicated, and placed aboard the *Erik*. The poor fellow's spirits commenced to rise immediately and there is good chance of his recovery and safe return home.

We learn that Dr. Cook, with two Esquimo boys, is over on the Grant Land side, and in probably desperate circumstances, if he is still alive. The Commander has issued orders in writing to Murphy and Billy Pritchard to be on the lookout for him and give him all the help he may need, and has also instructed the Esquimos to keep careful watch for any traces of him, while on their hunting trips.

There is a cache of Dr. Cook's provisions here, which Franke turned over to the Commander, and Mr. Whitney has agreed to help Murphy and Billy to guard it.

Mr. Harry Whitney is one of the party of men who came here on the *Erik* to hunt in this region, and he has decided to stay here at Etah for the winter and wait for a ship to take him out next summer. The other two members of the hunting-party, Mr. Larned and Mr. Norton, returned on the *Erik*. If Mr. Whitney had asked me my advice, I would not have suggested that he remain, because, although he has fine equipment, there will not be much sport in his experience, and there will be a great deal of roughness. He will have to become like the Esquimos and they will be practically his only companions. However, Mr. Whitney has had a talk with the Commander in the cabin of the *Roosevelt,* and the Commander has given his consent and best wishes. Mr. Whitney's supplies have been unloaded and some additions from the *Erik* made, and there is no reason to fear for his safety.

August 8, 1908: My forty-second birthday. I have not mentioned it to any one, and there's only one other besides myself who knows that to-day I am twice three times seven years of age. Seventeen years ago to-day, Commander Peary, hobbling about on his crutches with his right leg in a sling, insisted on giving me a birthday party. I was twenty-five years old then, and on the threshold of my Arctic experience. Never before in my life had the anniversary of my birth been celebrated, and to have a party given in my honor touched me deeply. Mrs. Peary was a member of the expedition then, and I suppose that it was due to her that the occasion was made a memorable one for me. Last year, I was aboard the *Roosevelt* in the shadow of the "Statue of Liberty" in New York Bay, and was treated to a pleasant surprise by my wife.

Commander Peary gave me explicit instructions to get Nipsangwah and Myah ashore as quick as the Creator would let them, but to be sure that their seven curs were kept aboard; these two huskies having exalted ideas as to their rights and privileges. Egingwah, or Karko as we knew him, and Koodlootinah and his family were to come aboard.

Acting under orders, I obeyed, but it was not a pleasant task. I have known men who needed dogs less to pay a great deal more for one pup than was paid to Nipsangwah for his pack of seven. The dogs are a valuable asset to this people and these two men were dependent on their little teams to a greater extent than on the plates and cups of tin which they received in exchange for them.

August 8–9, 1908: Have been trading with the natives without any trouble; they will give anything I want for anything that I have that they want. "It's a shame to take the money," or, as money is unknown up here and has no value, I should say that I should be ashamed to take such an advantage of them, but if I should stop to consider the freight-rates to this part of the world, no doubt a hatchet or a knife is worth just what it can be traded in for.

The ship has been rapidly littering up until it is now in a most perfect state of dirtiness, and in order to get the supplies from the *Erik,* coal, etc., the movable articles, dogs, Esquimos, etc., will have to be shifted and yours truly is helping.

The dogs have been landed on a small island in the bay, where they are safe and cannot run away, and they can have a glorious time, fighting and getting acquainted with each other. Some of the Esquimos' goods are ashore, some aboard the *Erik,* and the rest forward on the roof of the deck-house, while the *Roosevelt* is getting her coal aboard.

The loading of the meat and coal has been done by the crews of the ships, assisted and *hampered* by some of the Esquimos, and I have been walrus-hunting, and taxidermizing; that is, I have skinned a pair of walrus so that they can be stuffed and mounted. This job has been very carefully, and I think successfully, done and the skins have been towed ashore. The hearts, livers, and kidneys have been brought aboard and the meat is to be loaded to-morrow. Two boat-loads of bones have been rowed over to Dog Island for dog-food.

Coaling and stowing of whale-meat aboard the *Roosevelt* was finished at noon, August 15, and all day Sunday, August 16, all hands were at the job transferring to the *Erik* the boxes of provisions that were to be left at the cache at Etah. Bos'n Murphy and Billy Pritchard, the cabin-boy, are to stay as guard until the return of the *Roosevelt* next summer. A blinding storm of wind and snow prevented the *Roosevelt* from starting until about two-thirty P.M., when, with all the dogs a-howling, the whistle tooting, and the crew and members cheering, we steamed out of the Harbor into Smith Sound, and a thick fog which compelled half-speed past Littleton Island and into heavy pack-ice.

Captain Bartlett was navigating the ship and his eagle eye found a lane of open water from Cape Sabine to Bache Peninsula and open water from Ellesmere Land half-way across Buchanan Bay, but this lead closed on him, and the *Roosevelt* had to stop. Late in the evening, the ice started to move and grind alongside of the ship, but did no damage except scaring the Esquimos. Daylight still kept up and we went to sleep with our boots on!

From Etah to Cape Sheridan, which was to be our last point north in the ship, consumed twenty-one days of the hardest kind of work imaginable for a ship; actually fighting for every foot of the way against the almost impassable ice. For another ship it would have been impassable, but the *Roosevelt* was built for this kind of work, and her worth and ability had been proven on the voyage of 1905. The constant jolting, bumping, and jarring against the ice-packs, forwards and backwards, the sudden stops and starts and the frequent storms made work and comfort aboard ship all but impossible.

Had it been possible to be ashore at some point of vantage, to witness the struggles of our little ship against her giant adversaries would have been an impressive sight.

I will not dwell on the trying hours and days of her successful battle, the six days of watching and waiting for a chance to get out of our dangerous predicament in Lincoln Bay, the rounding of the different capes en route, or the horrible jams in Lady Franklin Bay. The good ship kept at the fight and won by sheer bulldogged tenacity and pluck. Life aboard her during those twenty-one days was not one sweet song, but we did not suffer unusually, and a great deal of necessary work was done on our equipment. The Esquimo women sewed diligently on the fur clothing we were to wear during the coming winter and I worked on the sledges that were to be used. Provisions were packed in compact shape and every one was busy. Two caches of provisions were made ashore in the event of an overland retreat, and the small boats were fully provisioned as a precaution against the loss of the ship. We did not dwell on the thought of losing it, but we took no chances.

Meeting with continual rebuffs, but persistently forging ahead and gaining deliberately day by day, the *Roosevelt* pushed steadily northward through the ice-encumbered waters of Kane Basin, Kennedy and Robeson Channels, and around the northeast corner of Grant Land to the shelter of Cape Sheridan, which was reached early in the afternoon of September 5, 1908.

CHAPTER IV

Preparing for Winter at Cape Sheridan—The Arctic Library

NOW THAT WE HAD REACHED Cape Sheridan in the ship, every one's spirits seemed to soar. It was still daylight, with the sun above the horizon, and although two parties had been landed for hunting, no one seemed to be in any particular hurry. The weather was cold but calm, and even in the rush of unloading the ship I often heard the hum of songs, and had it not been for the fur-jacketed men who were doing the work, it would not have been difficult for me to imagine myself in a much warmer climate.

Of course! in accordance with my agreement with some other members of this expedition I kept my eye on the Commander, and although it was not usual for him to break forth into song, I frequently heard him humming a popular air, and I knew that for the present all was well with him.

With the ship lightened, by being unloaded, to a large extent, of all of the stores, she did not very appreciably rise, but the Commander and the Captain agreed that she could be safely worked considerably closer to the shore, inside of the tide-crack possibly; and the *Roosevelt* was made fast to the ice-foot of the land, with a very considerable distance between her and open water. Her head was pointed due north, and affairs aboard her assumed regulation routine. The stores ashore were contracted, and work on getting them into shape for building temporary houses was soon under way. The boxes of provisions themselves formed the walls, and the roofing was made from makeshifts such as sails, overturned whale-boats, and rocks; and had the ship got adrift and been lost, the houses on shore would have proved ample and comfortable for housing the expedition.

A ship, and a good one like the *Roosevelt,* is the prime necessity in getting an expedition within striking distance of the Pole, but once here the ship (and no other boat but the *Roosevelt* could get here) is not indispensable, and accordingly all precautions against her loss were taken.

It is a fact that Arctic expeditions have lost their ships early in the season and in spite of the loss have done successful work. The last Ziegler Polar Expedition of 1903–1905 is an example. In the ship *America* they reached Crown Prince Rudolph Island on the European route, and shortly after landing, in the beginning of the long night, the *America* went adrift, and has never been seen since. It is not difficult to imagine her still drifting in the lonely Arctic Ocean, with not a soul aboard (a modern phantom ship in a sea of eternal ice). A more likely idea is that she has been crushed by the ice, and sunk, and the skeleton of her hulk strewn along the bottom of the sea, full many a fathom deep.

However, the depressing probabilities of the venture we are on are not permitted to worry us. The *Roosevelt* is a "Homer" and we confidently expect to have her take us back to home and loved ones.

In the meantime, I have a steady job carpentering, also interpreting, barbering, tailoring, dog-training, and chasing Esquimos out of my quarters. The Esquimos have the run of the ship and get everywhere except into the Commander's cabin, which they have been taught to regard as "The Holy of Holies." With the help of a sign which tersely proclaims "No Admittance," painted on a board and nailed over the door, they are without much difficulty restrained from going in.

The Commander's stateroom is a *state* room. He has a piano in there and a photograph of President Roosevelt; and right next door he has a private bath-room with a bath-tub in it. The bath-tub is chock-full of impedimenta of a much solider quality than water, but it is to be cleared out pretty soon, and every morning the Commander is going to have his cold-plunge, if there is enough hot water.

There is a general rule that every member of the expedition, including the sailors, must take a bath at least once a week, and it is wonderful how contagious bathing is. Even the Esquimos catch it, and frequently Charley has to interrupt the upward development of some ambitious native, who has suddenly perceived the need of ablutions, and has started to scrub himself in the water that is intended for cooking purposes. If the husky has not gone too far, the water is not wasted, and our stew is all the more savory.

On board ship there was quite an extensive library, especially on Arctic and Antarctic topics, but as it was in the

Commander's cabin it was not heavily patronized. In my own cabin I had Dickens' "Bleak House," Kipling's "Barrack Room Ballads," and the poems of Thomas Hood; also a copy of the Holy Bible, which had been given to me by a dear old lady in Brooklyn, N.Y. I also had Peary's books, "Northward Over the Great Ice," and his last work "Nearest the Pole." During the long dreary midnights of the Arctic winter, I spent many a pleasant hour with my books. I also took along with me a calendar for the years 1908 and 1909, for in the regions of noonday darkness and midnight daylight, a calendar is absolutely necessary.

But mostly I had rougher things than reading to do.

CHAPTER V

Making Peary Sledges—Hunting in the Arctic Night—
The Excitable Dogs and Their Habits

I HAVE BEEN BUSY MAKING SLEDGES, sledges of a different pattern from those used heretofore, and it is expected that they will answer better than the Esquimo type of open-work sledge, of the earlier expeditions. These sledges have been designed by Commander Peary and I have done the work.

The runners are longer, and are curved upwards at each end, so that they resemble the profile of a canoe, and are expected to rise over the inequalities of the ice much better than the old style. Lashed together with sealskin thongs, about twelve feet long, by two feet wide and seven inches high, the load can be spread along their entire length instead of being piled up, and a more even distribution of the weights is made. The Esquimos, used to their style of sledge, are of the opinion that the new style will prove too much for one man and an ordinary team to handle, but we have given both kinds a fair trial and it looks as if the new type has the old beaten by a good margin.

The hunting is not going along as successfully as is desired. The sun is sinking lower and lower, and the different hunting parties return with poor luck, bringing to the ship nothing in some cases, and in others only a few hares and some fish.

The Commander has told me that it is imperative that fresh meat be secured, and now that I have done all that it is positively necessary for me to do here at the ship, I am to take a couple of the Esquimo boys and try my luck for musk-oxen or reindeer, so to-morrow, early in the morning, it is off on the hunt.

This from my diary: Eight days out and not a shot, not a sight of game, nothing. The night is coming quickly, the long months of darkness, of quiet and cold, that, in spite of my years of experience, I can never get used to; and up here at Sheridan it comes sooner and lasts longer than it does down at Etah and Bowdoin Bay. Only a few days' difference, but it *is* longer, and I do not welcome it. Not a sound, except the report of a glacier, broken off by its weight, and causing a new iceberg to be born. The black darkness of the sky, the stars twinkling above, and hour after hour going by with no sunlight. Every now and then a moon when storms do not come, and always the cold, getting colder and colder, and me out on the hunt for fresh meat. I know it; the same old story, a man's work and a dog's life, and what does it amount to? What good is to be done? I am tired, sick, sore, and discouraged.

The main thing was game, but I had a much livelier time with some members of the Peary Arctic Club's expedition known as "our four-footed friends"—the dogs.

The dogs are ever interesting. They never bark, and often bite, but there is no danger from their bites. To get together a team that has not been tied down the night before is a job. You take a piece of meat, frozen as stiff as a piece of sheet-iron, in one hand, and the harness in the other, you single out the cur you are after, make proper advances, and when he comes sniffling and snuffling and all the time keeping at a safe distance, you drop the sheet-iron on the snow, the brute makes a dive, and you make a flop, you grab the nearest thing grabable—ear, leg, or bunch of hair—and do your best to catch his throat, after which, everything is easy. Slip the harness over the head, push the forepaws through, and there you are, one dog hooked up and harnessed. After licking the bites and sucking the blood, you tie said dog to a rock and start for the next one. It is only a question of time before you have your team. When you have them, leave them alone; they must now decide who is fit to be the king of the team, and so they fight, they fight and fight; and once they have decided, the king is king. A growl from him, or only a look, is enough, all obey, except the females, and the females have their way, for, true to type, the males never harm the females, and it is always the females who start the trouble.

The dogs when not hitched to the sledges were kept together in teams and tied up, both at the ship and while we were hunting. They were not allowed to roam at large, for past experience with these customers had taught us that nothing in the way of food was safe from the attack of Esquimo dogs. I have seen tin boxes that had been chewed open by dogs in order to get at the contents, tin cans of condensed milk being gnawed like a bone, and skin clothing being chewed up like so much gravy. Dog fights were hourly occurrences, and we lost a great many by the ravages of the mysterious Arctic disease, piblokto, which affects all dog life and frequently human life. Indeed, it looked for a time as if we should lose the whole pack, so rapidly did they die, but constant care and attention permitted us to save most of them, and the fittest survived.

Next to the Esquimos, the dogs are the most interesting subjects in the Arctic regions, and I could tell lots of tales to prove their intelligence and sagacity. These animals, more wolf than dog, have associated themselves with the human beings of this country as have their kin in more congenial places of the earth. Wide head, sharp nose, and pointed ears, thick wiry hair, and, in some of the males, a heavy mane; thick bushy tail, curved up over the back; deep chest and forelegs wide apart; a typical Esquimo dog is the picture of alert attention. They are as intelligent as any dog in civilization, and a thousand times more useful. They earn their own livings and disdain any of the comforts of life. Indeed it seems that when life is made pleasant for them they get sick, lie down, and die; and when out on the march, with no food for days, thin, gaunt skeletons of their former selves, they will drag at the traces of the sledges and by their uncomplaining conduct, inspire their human companions to keep on.

Without the Esquimo dog, the story of the North Pole, would remain untold; for human ingenuity has not yet devised any other means to overcome the obstacles of cold, storm, and ice that nature has placed in the way than those that were utilized on this expedition.

CHAPTER VI

The Peary Plan—A Rain of Rocks— My Friends the Esquimos

THE STORY OF THE WINTER at Cape Sheridan is a story unique in the experience of Arctic exploration. Usually it is the rule to hibernate as much as possible during the period of darkness, and the party is confined closely to headquarters. The Peary plan is different; and constant activity and travel were insisted on.

There were very few days when all of the members of the expedition were together, after the ship had reached her destination. Hunting parties were immediately sent out, for it was on the big game of the country that the expedition depended for fresh meat. Professor Marvin commenced his scientific work, and his several stations were all remote from headquarters; and all winter long, parties were sledging provisions, equipment, etc., to Cape Columbia, ninety-three miles northwest, in anticipation of the journey to the Pole. Those who remained at headquarters did not find life an idle dream. There was something in the way of work going on all of the time. I was away from the ship on two hunting trips of about ten days each, and while at headquarters, I shaped and built over two dozen sledges, besides doing lots of other work.

Naturally there were frequent storms and intense cold, and in regard to the storms of the Arctic regions of North Greenland and Grant Land, the only word I can use to describe them is "terrible," in the fullest meaning it conveys. The effect of such storms of wind and snow, or rain, is abject physical terror, due to the realization of perfect helplessness. I have seen rocks a hundred and a hundred and fifty pounds in weight picked up by the storm and blown for distances of ninety or a hundred feet to the edge of a precipice, and there of their own momentum go hurtling through space to fall in crashing fragments at the base. Imagine the effect of such a rainfall of death-dealing bowlders on the feelings of a little group of three or four, who have sought the base of the cliff for shelter. I have been there and I have seen one of my Esquimo companions felled by a blow from a rock eighty-four pounds in weight, which struck him fairly between the shoulder-blades, literally knocking the life out of him. I have been there, and believe me, I have been afraid. A hundred-pound box of supplies, taking an aërial joy ride, during the progress of a storm down at Anniversary Lodge in 1894, struck Commander Peary a glancing blow which put him out of commission for over a week. These mighty winds make it possible for the herbivorous animals of this region to exist. They sweep the snow from vast stretches of land, exposing the hay and dried dwarf-willows, that the hare, musk-oxen, and reindeer feed on.

The Esquimo families who came north to Cape Sheridan with us on the *Roosevelt* found life much more ideal than down in their native land. It was a pleasure trip for them, with nothing to worry about, and everything provided. Some of the families lived aboard ship all through the winter, and some in the boxhouse on shore. They were perforce much cleaner in their personal habits than they were wont to be in their own home country, but never for an instant does the odor or appearance of an Esquimo's habitation suggest the rose or geranium. The aroma of an East Side lunch-room is more like it.

There were thirty-nine Esquimos in the expedition, men, women and children; for the Esquimo travels heavy and takes his women and children with him as a matter of course. The women were as useful as the men, and the small boys did the ship's chores, sledging in fresh water from the lake, etc. They were mostly in families; but there were several young, unmarried men, and the unattached, much-married and divorced Miss "Bill," who domiciled herself aboard the ship and did much good work with her needle. She was my seamstress and the thick fur clothes worn on the trip to the Pole were sewn by her. The Esquimos lived as happily as in their own country and carried on their domestic affairs with almost the same care-free irregularity as usual. The best-natured people on earth, with no bad habits of their own, but a ready ability to assimilate the vices of civilization. Twenty years ago, when I first met them, not one used tobacco or craved it. To-day every member of the tribe has had experience with tobacco, craves it, and will give most everything, except his gun, to get it. Even little toddlers, three and four years old, will eat tobacco and, strange to say, it has no bad effect. They get tobacco from the Danish missionaries and from the sailors on board the whaling, seal, and walrus-ships. Whisky has not yet gotten in its demoralizing work.

It is my conviction that the life of this little tribe is doomed, and that extinction is nearly due. It will be caused partly by themselves, and partly by the misguided endeavors of civilized people. Every year their number diminishes; in 1894, Hugh J. Lee took the census of the tribe, and it numbered two hundred and fifty-three; in 1906, Professor Marvin found them to have dwindled to two hundred and seven. At this writing I dare say their number is still further reduced, for the latest news I have had from the Whale Sound region informs me that quite a number of deaths have occurred, and the birth-rate is not high. It is sad to think of the fate of my friends who live in what was once a land of plenty, but which is, through the greed of the commercial hunter, becoming a land of frigid desolation. The seals are practically gone, and the walrus are being quickly exterminated. The reindeer and the musk-oxen are going the same way, for the Esquimos themselves now hunt inland, when, up to twenty years ago, their hunting was confined to the coast and the life-giving sea.

They are very human in their attributes, and in spite of the fact that their diet is practically meat only, their tempers are gentle and mild, and there is a great deal of affection among them. Except between husband and wife, they seldom quarrel; and never hold spite or animosity. Children are a valuable asset, are much loved, never scolded or punished, and are not spoiled. An Esquimo mother washes her baby the same way a cat washes her kittens. There are lots of personal habits the description of which might scatter the reading circle, so I will desist with the bald statement, that, for them, dirt and filth have no terrors.

CHAPTER VII

Sledging to Cape Columbia—
Hot Soldering in Cold Weather

IF YOU WILL GET OUT your geography and turn to the map of the Western Hemisphere you will be able to follow me. Take the seventieth meridian, west. It is the major meridian of the Western Hemisphere, its northern land extremity being Cape Columbia, Grant Land; southward it crosses our own Cape Cod and the island of Santo Domingo, and runs down through the Andes to Cape Horn, the southern extremity of South America.

The seventieth meridian was our pathway to the Pole, based on the west longitude of 70°. Both Professor Marvin and Captain Bartlett took their observations at their respective farthests, and at the Pole, where all meridians meet, Commander Peary took his elevations of the sun, based on the local time of the Columbian meridian.

Cape Columbia was discovered over fifty yeas ago, by the intrepid Captain Hall, who gave his life to Arctic exploration, and lies buried on the Greenland coast. From the time of the arrival of the *Roosevelt* at Cape Sheridan, the previous September, communications with Cape Columbia were opened up, the trail was made and kept open all through the winter by constant travel between the ship and the cape. Loads of supplies, in anticipation of the start for the Pole, were sledged there.

The route to Cape Columbia is through a region of somber magnificence. Huge beetling cliffs overlook the pathway; dark savage headlands, around which we had to travel, project out into the ice-covered waters of the ocean, and vast stretches of wind-swept plains meet the eye in alternate changes. From Cape Sheridan to Cape Columbia is a distance of ninety-three miles. In ordinary weather, it took about three and a half marches, although on the return from the Pole it was covered in two marches, men and dogs breezing in.

On February 18, 1909, I left the *Roosevelt* on what might be a returnless journey. The time to strike had come. Captain Bartlett and Dr. Goodsell had already started. The Commander gave me strict orders to the effect that I must get to Porter Bay, pick up the cache of alcohol left there late in the previous week, solder up the leaks, and take it to Cape Columbia, there to await his arrival. The cause of the alcohol-leakage was due to the jolting of the sledges over the rough ice, puncturing the thin tin of the alcohol-cases.

I wish you could have seen me soldering those tins, under the conditions of darkness, intense cold, and insufficient furnace arrangement I had to endure. If there ever was a job for a demon in Hades, that was it. I vividly recall it. At the same instant I was in imminent danger of freezing to death and being burned alive; and the mental picture of those three fur-clad men, huddled around the little oil-stove heating the soldering-iron, and the hot solder dripping on the tin, is amusing now; but we were anything but amused then. The following is transcribed from my diary:

February 18, 1909: Weather clear, temperature 28° at five A.M. We were ready to leave the ship at seven-thirty A.M., but a blinding gale delayed our start until nine A.M. Two parties have left for Columbia: Professor MacMillan, three boys, four sledges, and twenty-four dogs; and my party of three boys and the same outfit. Each sledge is loaded with about two hundred and fifty pounds of provisions, consisting of pemmican, biscuits, tea, and alcohol. The Arctic night still holds sway, but to-day at noon, far to the south, a thin band of twilight shows, giving promise of the return of the sun, and every day now will increase in light. Heavy going to Porter Bay, where we are to spend the night, and as soon as rested start to work soldering up the thirty-six leaky alcohol tins left there by George Borup last week. Professor MacMillan and his party have not shown up yet. They dropped behind at Cape Richardson and we are keeping a watch for them. Snow still drifting and the wind howling like old times. Have had our evening meal of travel-rations; pemmican, biscuits, and tea and condensed milk, which was eaten with a relish. Two meals a day now, and big work between meals. No sign of Professor MacMillan and his crew, so we are going to turn in. The other igloo is waiting for him and the storm keeps up.

February 19, 1909: It was six A.M. when I routed out the boys for breakfast. I am writing while the tea is brewing. Had a good sleep last night when I did get to sleep. Snoring, talk about snoring! Sleeping with Esquimos on either side, who have already fallen asleep, is impossible. The only way to get asleep is to wake them up, get them good and wide-awake, inquire solicitously as to their comfort, and before they can get to sleep fall asleep yourself. After that, their rhythmic snores will only tend to soothe and rest you.

Worked all day soldering the tins of alcohol, and a very trying job it was. I converted the oil-stove into an alcohol-burner, and used it to heat the irons. It took some time for me to gauge properly the height above the blue flame of the alcohol at which I would get the best results in heating the irons, but at last we found it. A cradle-shaped support made from biscuit-can wire was hung over the flame about an inch above it, and while the boys heated the irons, I squatted on my knees with a case of alcohol across my lap and got to work. I had watched Mr. Wardwell aboard the ship solder up the cases and I found that watching a man work, and doing the same thing yourself, were two different matters. I tried to work with mittens on; I tried to work with them off. As soon as my bare fingers would touch the cold metal of the tins, they would freeze, and if I attempted to use the mittens they would singe and burn, and it was impossible to hold the solder with my bearskin gloves on. But keeping everlastingly at it brings success, and with the help of the boys the work was slowly but surely done.

Early this evening Professor MacMillan and his caravan arrived. He complimented me on the success of my work and informed me that they camped at Cape Richardson last night and that the trail had been pretty well blown over by the storm, but that the sledge-tracks were still to be seen. Dead tired, but not cold or uncomfortable. The stew is ready and so am I. Good night!

February 20: Wind died down, sky clear, and weather cold as usual. Our next point is Sail Harbor and after breakfast we set out. The Professor has asked me the most advisable way; whether to keep to the sea-ice or go overland, and we have agreed to follow the northern route, overland across Fielden Peninsula, using Peary's Path. By this route we estimate a saving of eight miles of going, and we will hit the beach at James Ross Bay.

Five P.M.: Sail Harbor. Stopped writing to eat breakfast, and then we loaded up and started. Reached here about an hour ago and from the fresh tracks in the snow, the Captain's or the Doctor's party have just recently left. It was evidently Doctor Goodsell and his crew who were here last; for Captain Bartlett left the *Roosevelt* on February 15 and the Doctor did not leave until the 16th. The going has been heavy, due to loose snow and heavy winds. Also intense cold; the thermometers are all out of commission, due to bubbles; but a frozen bottle of brandy proves that we had at least −45° of cold. The igloo I built last December 5 is the one my party are camped in. Professor MacMillan and his party kept up with us all day, and it was pleasant to have his society. Writing is difficult, the kettle is boiled, so here ends to-day's entry.

February 21: Easy wind, clear sky, but awful cold. Going across Clements Markham Inlet was fine, and we were able to steal a ride on the sledges most of the way, but we all had our faces frosted, and my short flat nose, which does not readily succumb to the cold, suffered as much as did MacMillan's. Even these men of iron, the Esquimos, suffered from the cold, Ootah freezing the great toe of his right foot. Perforce, he was compelled to thaw it out in the usual way; that is, taking off his kamik and placing his freezing foot under my bearskin shirt, the heat of my body thawing out the frozen member.

Cape Colan was reached about half past nine this morning. There we reloaded, and I fear overloaded, the sledges, from the cache which has been placed there. Our loads average about 550 pounds per sledge and we have left a lot of provisions behind.

We are at Cape Good Point, having been unable to make Cape Columbia, and have had to build an igloo. With our overloaded sledges this has been a hard day's work. The dogs pulled, and we pushed, and frequently lifted the heavily loaded sledges through the deep, soft snow; but we did not dump any of our loads. Although the boys wanted to, I would not stand for it. The bad example of seeing some piles of provision-cases which had been unloaded by the preceding parties was what put the idea in their heads.

We will make Cape Columbia to-morrow and will have to do no back-tracking. We are moving forward. I have started for a place, and do not intend to run back to get a better start.

February 22, 1909: Cape Columbia. We left Cape Good Point at seven A.M. and reached Cape Columbia at eight P.M. No wind, but weather thick and hazy, and the same old cold. About two miles from Good Point, we passed the Doctor's igloo. About a mile beyond this, we passed the "Crystal Palace" that had been occupied by the Captain. Six miles farther north, we passed a second igloo, which had been built by the Doctor's party. How did we know who had built and occupied these igloos? It was easy, as an Esquimo knows and recognizes another Esquimo's handwork, the same as you recognize the handwriting of your friends. I noted the neat, orderly, shipshape condition of the Captain's igloo, and the empty cocoa-tins scattered around the Doctor's igloo. The Doctor was the only one who had cocoa as an article of supply.

Following the trail four miles farther north, we passed the Captain's second igloo. He had unloaded his three sledges here and gone on to Parr Bay to hunt musk-oxen. We caught up with the Doctor and his party at the end of the ice-foot and pushed on to Cape Columbia. We found but one igloo here and I did the "after you my dear Alphonse," and the Doctor got the igloo. My boys and I have built a good big one in less than an hour, and we are now snug and warm.

CHAPTER VIII

In Camp at Columbia—Literary Igloos—The Magnificent Desolation of the Arctic

OUR HEAVY FURS had been made by the Esquimo women on board the ship and had been thoroughly aired and carefully packed on the sledges. We were to discard our old clothes before leaving the land and endeavor to be in the cleanest condition possible while contending with the ice, for we knew that we would get dirty enough without having the discomfort of vermin added. It is easy to become vermin-infested, and when all forms of life but man and dog seem to have disappeared, the bedbug still remains. Each person had taken a good hot bath with plenty of soap and water before we left the ship, and we had given each other what we called a "prize-fighter's hair-cut." We ran the clippers from forehead back, all over the head, and we looked like a precious bunch but we had hair enough on our heads by the time we came back from our three months' journey, and we needed a few more baths and new clothes.

When I met Dr. Goodsell at Cape Columbia, about a week after he had left the ship, he had already raised quite a beard, and, as his hair was black and heavy, it made quite a change in his appearance. The effect of the long period of darkness had been to give his complexion a greenish-yellow tinge. My complexion reminded him of a ginger cake with too much saleratus in it.

February 23: Heavy snow-fall but practically no wind this morning at seven o'clock, when Dr. Goodsell left his igloo for Cape Colan to pick up the load he had left there when he lightened his sledges, also some loads of pemmican and biscuits that had been cached. We had supper together and also breakfast this morning, and as we ate we laughed and talked, and I taught him a few tricks for keeping himself warm.

In spite of the snow, which was still falling, I routed out my boys, and in the dark we left camp for the western side of the cape, to get the four sledge-loads of rations that had been taken there the previous November. Got the loads and pushed south to Cape Aldrich, which is a point on the promontory of Cape Columbia. From Cape Aldrich the Commander intends to attack the sea-ice.

After unloading the supplies on the point, we came back to camp at Cape Columbia. Shortly afterwards Captain Bartlett came into camp from his musk-ox-hunt around Parr Bay. He had not shot a thing and was very tired and discouraged, but I think he was glad to see me. He was so hungry that I gave him all the stew, which he swallowed whole.

MacMillan and his party showed up about an hour after the Captain, and very shortly after George Borup came driving in, like "Ann Eliza Johnson, a swingin' down the line." I helped Mr. Borup build his igloo, for which he was grateful. He is a plucky young fellow and is always cheerful. He told us that Professor Marvin, according to the schedule, had left the ship on the 20th, and the Commander on the 21st, so they must be well on the way.

While waiting in this camp for the Commander and Professor Marvin to arrive, we had plenty of work; re-adjusting the sledge-loads and also building snow-houses and banking them with blocks of snow, for the wind had eroded one end of my igloo and completely razed it to the level of the ground, and a more solidly constructed igloo was necessary to withstand the fury of the gale.

We kept a fire going in one igloo and dried our mittens and kamiks. Though the tumpa, tumpa, plunk of the banjo was not heard, and our camp-fires were not scenes of revelry and joy, I frequently did the double-shuffle and an Old Virginia break-down, to keep my blood circulating.

The hours preceding our advance from Cape Columbia were pleasantly spent, though we lost no time in literary debates. There were a few books along.

Out on the ice of the Polar ocean, as far as reading matter went, I think Dr. Goodsell had a very small set of Shakespeare, and I know that I had a Holy Bible. The others who went out on the ice may have had reading matter with them, but they did not read it out loud, and so I am not in a position to say what their literary tastes were.

Even on shipboard, we had no pigskin library or five-foot shelf of sleep-producers, but each member had some favorite books in his cabin, and they helped to form a circulating library.

WHILE WE WAITED here, we had time to appreciate the magnificent desolation about us. Even on the march, with loaded sledges and tugging dogs to engage attention, unconsciously one finds oneself with wits wool-gathering and eyes taking in the scene, and suddenly being brought back to the business of the hour by the fiend-like conduct of his team.

There is an irresistible fascination about the regions of northernmost Grant Land that is impossible for me to describe. Having no poetry in my soul, and being somewhat hardened by years of experience in that inhospitable country, words proper to give you an idea of its unique beauty do not come to mind. Imagine gorgeous bleakness, beautiful blankness. It never seems broad, bright day, even in the middle of June, and the sky has the different effects of the varying hours of morning and evening twilight from the first to the last peep of day. Early in February, at noon, a thin band of light appears far to the southward, heralding the approach of the sun, and daily the twilight lengthens, until early in March, the sun, a flaming disk of fiery crimson, shows his distorted image above the horizon. This distorted shape is due to the mirage caused by the cold, just as heat-waves above the rails on a railroad-track distort the shape of objects beyond.

The south sides of the lofty peaks have for days reflected the glory of the coming sun, and it does not require an artist to enjoy the unexampled splendor of the view. The snows covering the peaks show all of the colors, variations, and tones of the artist's palette, and more. Artists have gone with us into the Arctic and I have heard them rave over the wonderful beauties of the scene, and I have seen them at work trying to reproduce some of it, with good results but with nothing like the effect of the original. As Mr. Stokes said, "it is color run riot."

To the northward, all is dark and the brighter stars of the heavens are still visible, but growing fainter daily with the strengthening of the sunlight.

When the sun finally gets above the horizon and swings his daily circle, the color effects grow less and less, but then the sky and cloud-effects improve and the shadows in the mountains and clefts of the ice show forth their beauty, cold blues and grays; the bare patches of the land, rich browns; and the whiteness of the snow is dazzling. At midday, the optical impression given by one's shadow is of about nine o'clock in the morning, this due to the altitude of the sun, always giving us long shadows. Above us the sky is blue and bright, bluer than the sky of the Mediterranean, and the clouds from the silky cirrus mare's-tails to the fantastic and heavy cumulus are always objects of beauty. This is the description of fine weather.

Almost any spot would have been a fine one to get a round of views from; at Cape Sheridan, our headquarters, we were bounded by a series of land marks that have become historical; to the north, Cape Hecla, the point of departure of the 1906 expedition; to the west, Cape Joseph Henry, and beyond, the twin peaks of Cape Columbia rear their giant summits out to the ocean.

From Cape Columbia the expedition was now to leave the land and sledge over the ice-covered ocean four hundred and thirteen miles north—to the Pole!

CHAPTER IX

Ready for the Dash to the Pole—
The Commander's Arrival

THE DIARY—FEBRUARY 23: Heavy snow-fall and furious winds; accordingly intense darkness and much discomfort.

There was a heavy gale blowing at seven o'clock in the morning, on February 22, and the snow was so thick and drifty that we kept close to our igloos and made no attempt to do more than feed the dogs. My igloo was completely covered with snow and the one occupied by Dr. Goodsell was blown away, so that he had to have another one, which I helped to build.

The wind subsided considerably, leaving a thick haze, but after breakfast, Professor MacMillan, Mr. Borup, and their parties, left camp for Cape Colan, to get the supplies they had dumped there, and carry them to Cape Aldrich. I took one Esquimo, Pooadloonah, and one sledge from the Captain's party, and with my own three boys, Ooblooyah, Ootah, and

I-forget-his-name, and a howling mob of dogs, we left for the western side of Cape Columbia, and got the rest of the pemmican and biscuits. On the way back, we met the Captain, who was out taking exercise. He had nothing to say; he did not shake hands, but there was something in his manner to show that he was glad to see us. With the coming of the daylight a man gets more cheerful, but it was still twilight when we left Cape Columbia, and melancholy would sometimes grip, as it often did during the darkness of midwinter.

Captain Bartlett helped us to push the loaded sledges to Cape Aldrich and nothing was left at Cape Columbia.

When we got back to camp we found Professor Marvin and his party of three Esquimos there. They had just reached the camp and were at work building an igloo.

Professor Marvin came over to our igloo and changed his clothes; that is, in a temperature of at least 45° below zero, by the light of my lantern he coolly and calmly stripped to the pelt, and proceeded to clothe himself in the new suit of reindeerskin and polar bearskin clothing, that had been made for him by the Esquimo woman, Ahlikahsingwah, aboard the *Roosevelt*. It had taken him and his party five days to make the trip from Sheridan to Columbia.

February 26: This from my log: "Clear, no wind, temperature 57° below zero." Listen! I will tell you about it. At seven A.M. we quit trying to sleep and started the pot a-boiling. A pint of hot tea gave us a different point of view, and Professor Marvin handed me the thermometer, which I took outside and got the reading; 57° below; that is cold enough. I have seen it lower, but after forty below the difference is not appreciable.

I climbed to the highest pinnacle of the cape and in the gathering daylight gazed out over the ice-covered ocean to get an idea of its condition. At my back lay the land of sadness, just below me the little village of snow-houses, the northern-most city on the earth (Commander Peary gave it the name Crane City), and, stretching wide and far to the northward, the irresistible influence that beckoned us on; broken ice, a sinister chaos, through which we would have to work our way. Dark and heavy clouds along the horizon gave indication of open water, and it was easy to see that the rough and heavy shore-ice would make no jokes for us to appreciate.

About an hour or so after the midday meal, a loud outcry from the dogs made me go outside to see what was up. This was on the afternoon of February 26. I quickly saw what the dogs were excited about.

With a "Whoop halloo," three Komaticks were racing and tearing down the gradient of the land to our camp, and all of us were out to see the finish. Kudlooktoo and Arkeo an even distance apart; and heads up, tails up, a full five sledge-lengths ahead, with snowdust spinning free, the dog-team of the ever victorious Peary in the lead. The caravan came to a halt with a grandstand finish that it would have done you good to witness.

The Commander didn't want to stop. He immediately commenced to shout and issue orders, and, by the time he had calmed down, both Captain Bartlett and George Borup had loaded up and pushed forward on to the ice of the Arctic Ocean, bound for the trophy of over four hundred years of effort. The Peary discipline is the iron hand ungloved. From now on we must be indifferent to comfort, and like poor little Joe in "Bleak House" we must always be moving on.

CHAPTER X

Forward! March!

COMMANDER PEARY WAS an officer of the United States Navy, but there never was the slightest military aspect to any of his expeditions. No banners flying, no trumpets blaring, and no sharp, incisive commands. Long ago, crossing the ice-cap of North Greenland, he carried a wand of bamboo, on one end of which was attached a little silk guidon, with a star embroidered on it, but even that had been discarded and the only thing military about this expedition was his peremptory "Forward! March!" What flags we had were folded and stowed on Commander Peary's sledge, and broken-out only at the North Pole.

Captain Bartlett and Mr. George Borup were all alert and at attention, the command of preparation and the command of execution were quickly given in rapid succession, and they were off.

From the diary.

February 28, 1909: A bright, clear morning. Captain Bartlett and his crew, Ooqueah, Pooadloonah, and Harrigan; and George Borup and Karko, Seegloo, and Keshungwah, have set sail and are on their way.

Captain Bartlett made the trail and George Borup was the scout, and a rare "Old Scout" he was. He kept up the going for three days and then came back to the land to start again with new loads of supplies.

The party that stayed at Crane City until March 1 consisted of Commander Peary, MacMillan, Goodsell, Marvin, myself, and fourteen Esquimos, whom you don't know, and ninety-eight dogs, that you may have heard about.

The dogs were double-fed and we put a good meal inside ourselves before turning-in on the night of February 28, 1909. The next morning was to be our launching, and we went to sleep full of the thought of what was before us. From now on it was keep on going, and keep on—and we kept on; sometimes in the face of storms of wind and snow that it is impossible for you to imagine.

Day does not break in the Arctic regions, it just comes on quietly the same as down here, but I must say that at daybreak on March 1, 1909, we were all excitement and attention. A furious wind was blowing, which we took as a good omen; for, on all of Commander Peary's travelings, a good big, heavy storm of blinding snow has been his stirrup-cup and here he had his last. Systematically we had completed our preparations on the two days previous, so that, by six A.M. of the 1st of March, we were ready and standing at the upstanders of our sledges, awaiting the command "Forward! March!"

Already, difficulties had commenced. Ooblooyah and Slocum (Esquimo name, Inighito, but, on account of his dilatory habits, known as Slocum) were incapacitated;

Ooblooyah with a swelled knee, and Slocum with a frozen heel. The cold gets you in most any place, up there.

I and my three boys were ordered to take the lead. We did so, at about half past six o'clock in the morning. Forward! March! and we were off.

Previous page: Matthew Henson immediately after the return sledge trip from the Pole, 1909.
This page: A young Matt Henson in uniform; Henson in 1907; Henson and Peary, c. 1901.

Matt Henson

Top: Henson in Nicaragua, 1887.
Bottom: Peary and Henson in Nicaragua.

Henson posing for publicity shots for the original edition of *A Negro Explorer at the North Pole*, 1912.

Henson in full Arctic parka, 1909.

Left: Henson modeling his furs after returning to the United States.
Right: Peary aboard the *Roosevelt*.

Henson feeding the sled dogs aboard ship.

Henson aboard ship.

Top: Henson relaxing aboard ship.
Bottom: Henson with 1909 expedition members Captain Robert Bartlett, George Borup, and Donald MacMillan.

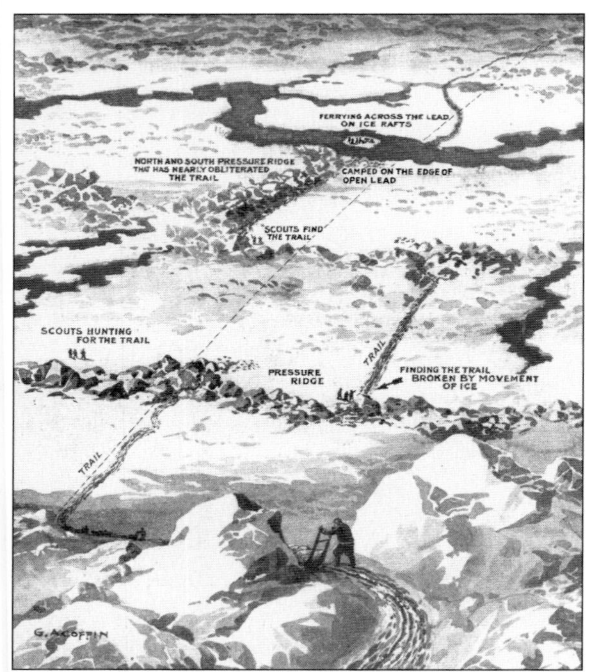

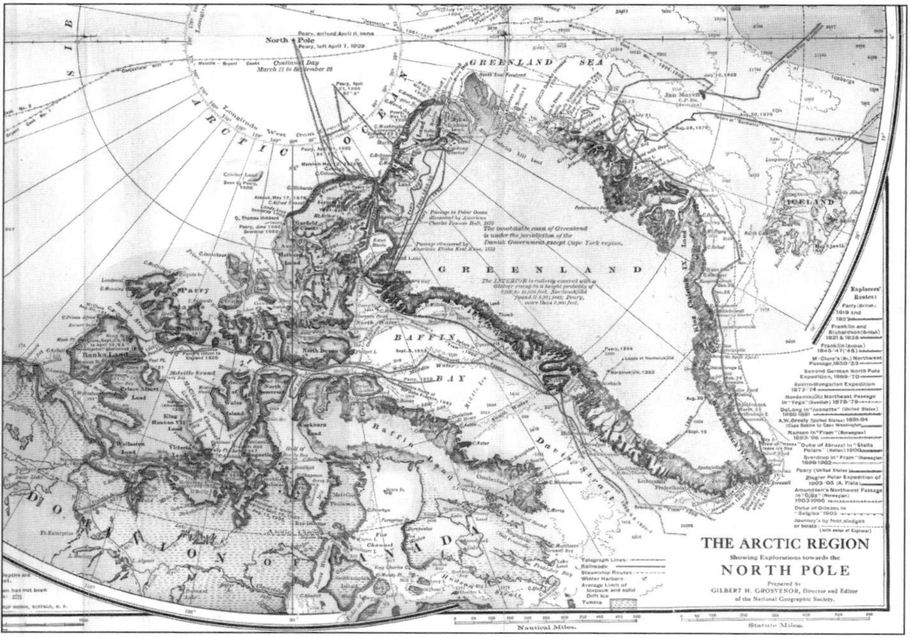

THE ARCTIC REGION
Showing Explorations towards the
NORTH POLE
Prepared by
GILBERT H. GROSVENOR, Director and Editor
of the National Geographic Society.

The route to the Pole.

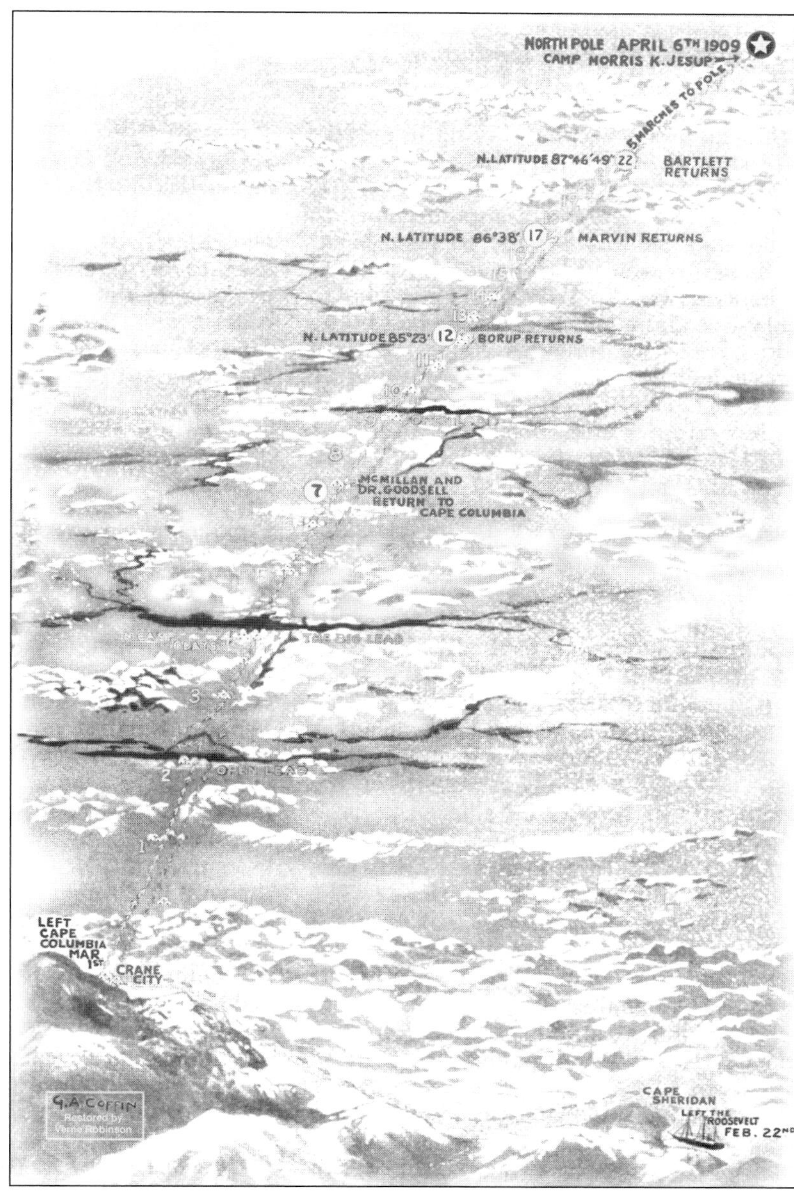
NORTH POLE APRIL 6TH 1909
CAMP MORRIS K. JESUP
5 MARCHES TO POLE
N. LATITUDE 87°46'49" 22
BARTLETT RETURNS
N. LATITUDE 86°38' 17
MARVIN RETURNS
N. LATITUDE 85°23' 12
BORUP RETURNS
MCMILLAN AND DR. GOODSELL RETURN TO CAPE COLUMBIA
THE BIG LEAD
OPEN LEAD
LEFT CAPE COLUMBIA MAR 1ST
CRANE CITY
CAPE SHERIDAN
LEFT THE ROOSEVELT FEB. 22ND
G.A. COFFIN
Restored by Verne Robinson

Henson holding a baby musk ox; eskimos skinning a polar bear; and Eskimos with one of the polar sleds.

Top: Double team of sled dogs at the Pole.
Bottom: Artist's rendition of the *Roosevelt* in ice.

Top: The *Roosevelt* at Cape Sheridan.
Bottom: Drying the sails for winter storage, 1908.

Top: Peary paying Eskimo women for making clothing for the expedition.
Bottom: Henson posing with the Eskimos.

Top: Sledge used to reach the Pole.
Bottom: Surveying the polar ice.

Top: The deadly business of crossing a lead.
Bottom: The sled train to the Pole.

Stopping for lunch the day before reaching the Pole.

Top: Building an igloo.
Bottom: Camp Morris K. Jesup at the North Pole.

Henson (center) and the four Eskimos beneath the Stars and Stripes at the North Pole.

Henson (center) and the Eskimos after reaching the Pole.

EGINGWAH BEFORE STARTING ON THE SLEDGE TRIP

EGINGWAH AFTER THE RETURN FROM THE TRIP

OOTAH BEFORE STARTING ON THE SLEDGE TRIP

OOTAH AFTER THE RETURN FROM THE SLEDGE TRIP

Egingwah and Ootah before and after the expedition.

Eskimo mother and child.

Eskimo children.

Top: Ahnighito ("the tent"), the 34-ton meteorite discovered by Peary's 1894 Greenland expedition.
Bottom: Henson at the Explorers' Club, c. 1947.

Henson demonstrating a snowshoe he wore on his Arctic expeditions.

Henson tells children in Harlem about his adventures, 1947.

Henson at age 81 with Navy medal.

Top: Henson and his wife visit President Eisenhower
in the White House, 1954.
Bottom: the Henson monument in Arlington National Cemetary,
designed by S. Allen Counter.

"Matt the kind one."

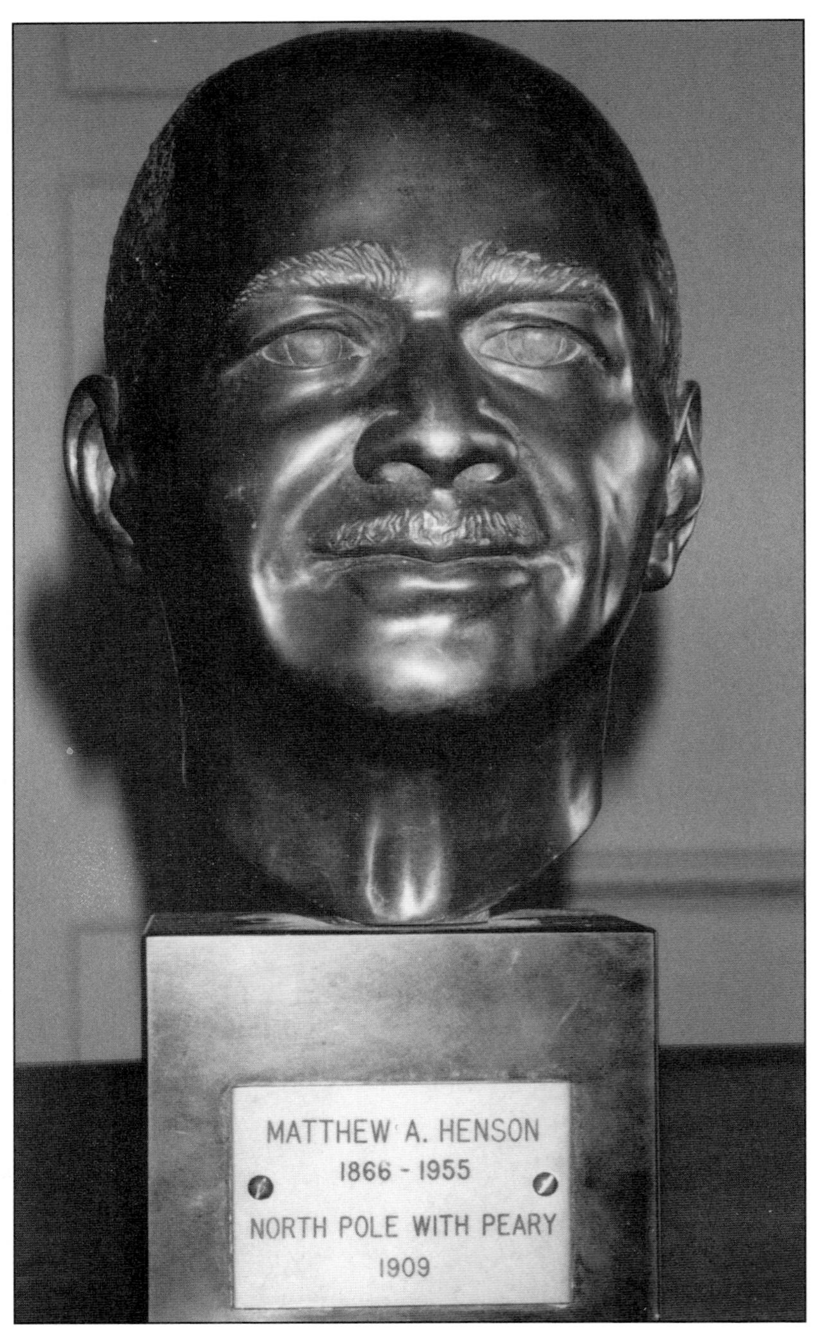

Bronze bust of Henson in the Explorers' Club.

CHAPTER XI

Fighting up the Polar Sea—Held up by the "Big Lead"

FOLLOWING THE TRAIL MADE by Captain Bartlett, we pushed off, every man at the upstander of his sledge to urge his team by whip and voice. It was only when we had perfect going over sheets of young ice that we were able to steal a ride on the sledges.

The trail led us over the glacial fringe for a quarter of a mile, and the going was fairly easy, but, after leaving the land ice-foot, the trail plunged into ice so rough that we had to use pickaxes to make a pathway. It took only about one mile of such going, and my sledge split.

"Number one," said I to myself, and I came to a halt. The gale was still blowing, but I started to work on the necessary repairs. I have practically built one sledge out of two broken ones, while out on the ice and in weather almost as bad as this; and I have almost daily during the journey had to repair broken sledges, sometimes under fiercer conditions; and so I will describe this one job and hereafter, when writing about repairing a sledge, let it go at that.

Cold and windy. Undo the lashings, unload the load, get out the brace and bit and bore new holes, taking plenty of time, for, in such cold, there is danger of the steel bit breaking. Then, with ungloved hands, thread the sealskin thongs through the hole. The fingers freeze. Stop work, pull the hand through the sleeve, and take your icy fingers to your heart; that is, put your hand under your armpit, and when you feel it burning you know it has thawed out. Then start to work again. By this time the party has advanced beyond you and, as orders are orders, and you have been ordered to take the lead, you have to start, catch up, and pass the column before you have reached your station.

Of course, in catching up and overtaking the party, you have the advantage of the well-marked trail they have made. Once again in the lead; and my boy, Ootah, had to up and break his sledge, and there was some more tall talking when the Commander caught up with us and left us there mending it. A little farther on, and the amiable Kudlooktoo, who was in my party at the time, busted his sledge. You would have thought that Kudlooktoo was the last person in Commander Peary's estimation, when he got through talking to him and telling him what he thought of him. The sledge was so badly broken it had to be abandoned. The load was left on the spot where the accident happened, and Kudlooktoo, much chastened and crestfallen, drove his team of dogs back to the land for a new sledge.

We did not wait for him, but kept on for about two hours longer, when we reached the Captain's first igloo, twelve miles out; a small day's traveling, but we were almost deadbeat, from having battled all day with the wind, which had blown a full-sized gale. No other but a Peary party would have attempted to travel in such weather. Our breath was frozen to our hoods of fur and our cheeks and noses frozen. Spreading our furs upon the snow, we dropped down and endeavored to sleep, but sound sleep was impossible. It was a night of Plutonian Purgatory. All through the night I would wake from the cold and beat my arms or feet to keep the circulation going, and I would hear one or both of my boys doing the same. I did not make any entries in the diary that day, and there was many a day like it after that.

It was cold and dark when we left camp number one on the morning of March 2, at half past six o'clock. Breakfast had warmed us up a bit, but the hard pemmican had torn and cut the roofs and sides of our mouths so that we did not eat a full meal, and we decided that at our next camp we would boil the pemmican in the tea and have a combination stew. I will say now that this experiment was tried, but it made such an unwholesome mess that it was never repeated.

The Captain's and Borup's trail was still evident, in spite of the low drifts of the snow, but progress was slow. We were still in the heavy rubble-ice and had to continuously hew our way with pickaxes to make a path for the sledges. While we were at work making a pathway, the dogs would curl up and lie down with their noses in their tails, and we would have to come back and start them, which was always the signal for a fight or two. We worked through the belt of rubble-ice at last, and came up with the heavy old floes and rafters of ice-blocks, larger than very large flagstones and fully as thick as they were long and wide; the fissures between them full of the drifted snow. Even with our broad snow-shoes on, we sank knee-deep, and the dogs were in up to their breasts, the sledges up to the floors and frequently turning over, so it was a long time before we had covered seven miles, to be stopped by open water. I took no chances on this lead, although afterwards I did not hesitate at more desperate-looking leads than this was. Instead of ferrying across on a block of ice, I left one of my boys to attend the dogs and sledges, and with Ootah I started to reconnoiter. We found that there were two leads, and the safest way to cross the first was to go west to a point where the young ice was strong enough to bear the weight of the sledges. We got across and had not gone very far before the other lead, in spite of a detour to the east, effectually blocked us. Starting back to the sledges, Ootah said he was *"damn feel good,"* and in Esquimo gave me to understand that he was going back to the ship. I tried to tell him different, as we walked back; and when we reached camp we found the Commander and his party, who had just come in; and the Commander gave Ootah to distinctly understand that he was not going back just yet. Orders were given to camp, and while the igloos were being built, Marvin and MacMillan took soundings. There had been more daylight than on the day before, and the gale had subsided considerably, but it was dark when we turned in to have our evening meal and sleep.

March 3: Right after breakfast, my party immediately started, taking the trail I had found the day previous. Examining the ice, we went to the westward, until we came to the almost solid new ice, and we took a chance. The ice commenced to rafter under us, but we got across safely with our loads, and started east again, for two miles; when we found ourselves on an island of ice completely surrounded by the heavy raftered ice. Here we halted and mended sledges and in the course of an hour the whole party had caught up. The ice had begun to rafter and the shattering reports made a noise that was almost ear-splitting, but we pushed and pulled and managed to get out of the danger-zone, and kept going northwestward, in the hope of picking up the trail of the Captain and Borup, which we did after a mile of going. Close examination of the trail showed us that Borup and his party had retraced their steps and gone quite a distance west in order to cross the lead. It was on this march that we were to have met Borup and his party returning, so Marvin and his boy Kyutah were sent to look them up. The rest of the party kept on in the newly found trail and came to the igloo and cache that had been left there by Borup. The Commander went into the igloo, and we made the dogs fast and built our own igloos, made our tea and went to sleep.

March 4: Heavy snow-fall; but Commander Peary routed out all hands, and by seven o'clock we were following the Captain's trail. Very rough going, and progress slow up to about nine o'clock, when conditions changed. We reached heavy, old floes of waving blue ice, the best traveling on sea-ice I had ever encountered in eighteen years' experience. We went so fast that we more than made up for lost time and at two o'clock, myself in the lead, we reached the igloo built by Captain Bartlett. It had been arranged that I should stop for one sleep at every igloo built by the Captain, and that he should leave a note in his igloo for my instructions; but, in spite of these previous arrangements, I felt that with such good traveling it would be just as wise to keep on going, and so we did, but it was only about half or three-quarters of an hour later when we were stopped by a lead, beside which the Captain had camped. With Ootah and Tommy to help, we built an igloo and crawled inside. Two hours later, the Commander and his party arrived, and we crawled out and turned the igloo over to him. Tommy, Ootah, and I then built another igloo, crawled inside, and blocked the doorway up with a slab of snow, determined not to turn out again until we had had a good feed and snooze.

From my diary, the first entry since leaving the land; with a couple of comments added afterwards:

March 5: A clear bright morning, 20° below zero; quite comfortable. Reached here yesterday at two-forty-five P.M., after some of the finest going I have ever seen. Commander Peary, Captain Bartlett, and Dr. Goodsell here, and fourteen Esquimos. First view of the sun to-day, for a few minutes at noon, makes us all cheerful. It was a crimson sphere, just balanced on the brink of the world. Had the weather been favorable, we could have seen the sun several days earlier. Every day following he will get higher and higher, until he finally swings around the sky above the horizon for the full twenty-four hours.

Early in the morning of the 5th, Peary sent a detachment of three Esquimos, in charge of MacMillan, back to bring in Borup's cache, left by him at the point where he turned back to return to the land for more loads. This detachment was back in camp by four o'clock in the afternoon of the same day. Nothing left to do but to rearrange the loads and wait for the lead to close.

The land is still in sight. Professor Marvin has gone back with two boys and is expected to keep on to the alcohol cache at Cape Columbia, turn back, and meet us here, or, if the ice freezes, to follow us until he catches up with us. We are husbanding our fuel, and two meals a day is our programme. We are still south of the Big Lead of 1906, but to all intents and purposes this is it. I am able to recognize many of the characteristics of it, and I feel sure it is the same old lead that gave us many an anxious hour in our upward and downward journey three years ago.

Fine weather, but we are still south of the 84th parallel and this open water marks it. 8° below zero and all comfortable. We should be doing twenty or twenty-five miles a day good traveling, but we are halted by this open water.

March 7: Professor MacMillan came into camp to-day with the cache he had picked up. There was quite a hullabaloo among the boys, and a great deal of argument as to who owned various articles of provender and equipment that had been brought into camp by MacMillan, and even I was on the point of jumping into the fracas in order to see fair play, until a wink from MacMillan told me that it was simply a put-up job of his to disconcert the Esquimos. Confidentially and on the side he has been dressing his heel, which in spite of all keeps on freezing, and is in very bad shape. His kamiks stick to the loose flesh and the skin will not form. All of the frost has been taken out, but I think skin-grafting is the only thing that will cure it. He wants to keep on going and asks me how far we have gone and wants to know if he shall tell Commander Peary about his injury. I have advised him to make a clean breast of it, but he feels good for a week or so more, and it is up to him.

We eat, and sleep, and watch the lead, and wonder. Are we to be repulsed again? Is the unseen, mysterious guardian of this mist-covered region foiling us? The Commander is taking it with a great deal more patience than he usually has with obstacles, but in the face of this one he probably realizes the necessity of a calm, philosophic mood.

Captain Bartlett has been here longer than any of us, and he is commencing to get nervous. Commander Peary and he have done what is nautically known as "swinging the ship," for the purpose of correcting compass errors, and after that there is nothing for them to do but wait. Captain Bartlett describes it as "Hell on Earth"; the Commander has nothing to say, and I agree with him. Dr. Goodsell reads from his little books, studies Esquimo language, writes in his diary and talks to me and the rest of the party, and waits.

Professor MacMillan, with his eye ever to the south, and an occasional glance at his frozen heel, cracks a joke and bids us be cheerful. He is one *man,* and has surely made good. His first trip to this forsaken region, yet he wakes up from his sleep with a smile on his face and a question as to how a nice, large, juicy steak would go about now. This is no place for jokes, yet his jokes are cheering and make us all feel more light-hearted. He is the "life of the funeral" and by his cheerfulness has kept our spirits from sinking to a dead level, and when the Esquimos commenced to get cranky, by his diplomacy he brought them to think of other subjects than going back to the ship.

He has started to kid us along by instituting a series of competitions in athletic endeavors, and the Esquimos fall for it like the Innocents that they are, and that is the object he is after. They have tried all of their native stunts, wrestling, boxing, thumb-pulling, and elbow-tests; and each winner has been awarded a prize. Most of the prizes are back on the ship and include the anchors, rudders, keel, and spars. Everything else has long since been given away, and these people have keen memories.

The Big Lead has no attraction for the Esquimos and the waiting for a chance to cross it has given them much opportunity to complain of cold feet. It is fierce, listening to their whines and howls. Of all yellow-livered curs deliver me. We have the best Esquimos in the tribe with us, and expect them to remain steadfast and loyal, but after they have had time to realize their position, the precariousness of it begins to magnify and they start in to whimper, and beg to be allowed to go back. They remember the other side of this damnable open water and what it meant to get back in 1906. I do not blame them, but I have had the Devil's own time in making my boys and some of the others see it the way the Commander wants us to look at it.

Indeed, two of the older ones, Panikpah and Pooadloonah, became so fractious that the Commander sent them back, with a written order to Gushue on the ship, to let them pack up their things and take their families and dogs back to Esquimo land, which they did. When the *Roosevelt* reached Etah the following August, on her return, these two men were there, fat and healthy, and merrily greeted us. No hard feelings whatever.

March 10: We could have crossed to-day, but there was a chance of Marvin and Borup catching up with their loads of alcohol, etc. Whether they catch up or not, to-morrow, early, we start across, and the indications are that the going will be heavy, for the ice is piled in rafters of pressure-ridges.

IT WAS EXASPERATING; seven precious days of fine weather lost; and fine weather is the exception, not the rule, in the Arctic. Here we were resting in camp, although we were not extremely tired and nowhere near exhausted. We were ready and anxious to travel on the 5th, next morning after we reached the Big Lead, but were perforce compelled to inaction. And so did we wait for nearly seven days beside that lead, before conditions were favorable for a crossing.

But early in the morning of March 11th the full party started; through the heaviest of going imaginable. Neither Borup nor Marvin had caught up, but we felt that unless something had happened to them, they would surely catch up in a few more days.

CHAPTER XII

Pioneering the Way—Breaking Sledges

MARCH 11, 1909: Clear, –45°. Off we go! Marvin and Borup have not yet shown up, but the lead is shut and the orders since yesterday afternoon have been to stand by for only twelve hours more; and while the tea is brewing I am using the warmth to write. We could have crossed thirty hours ago, but Commander Peary would not permit us to take chances; he wants to keep the party together as long as possible, and expects to have to send at least eight men back after the next march. MacMillan is not fit, and there are four or five of the natives who should be sent away. Three Esquimos apiece are too many, and I think Commander Peary is about ready to split the different crews of men and dogs. He himself is in very good shape and, due to his example, Captain Bartlett has again taken the field. A heavy storm of wind and snow is in progress, but the motion of the ice remains satisfactory.

This is not a regular camp. We are sheltered north of a huge paleocrystic floeberg; and the dogs are at rest, with their noses in their tails. Dr. Goodsell has set his boys to work building an igloo, which will not be needed, for I see Ooqueah and Egingwah piling up the loads on their sledges, and Professor MacMillan is very busy with his own personal sledge. No halt, only a breathing spell and, as I have predicted, we are on our way again. This is an extremely dangerous zone to halt or hazard in. The ice is liable to open here at any moment and let us either sink in the cold, black water or drift on a block of frozen ice, much too thin to enable us to get on to the heavy ice again. Three miles wide at least.

The foregoing was written while out on the ice of the Arctic Ocean, just after crossing the raftered hummocks of the ice of the Big Lead. While we were waiting for the rest of the expedition to gather in, I slumped down behind a peak of land or paleocrystic ice, and made the entry in my diary. We were not tired out; we had had more than six days' rest at the lead; and when it closed we pushed on across the pressure-ridges on to the heavy and cumbrous ice of the circumpolar sea. We were sure that we had passed the main obstruction, and in spite of the failure of Marvin and Borup to come in with the essentials of fuel-alcohol and food, Commander Peary insisted on pushing forward.

Prof. Donald B. MacMillan was with the party, but Commander Peary knew, without his telling him, that he was really no longer fit to travel, and Dr. Goodsell was not as far north of the land as original plans intended, so when both MacMillan and Goodsell were told that they must start back to the ship, I was not surprised.

It was on March 14 that the first supporting-party finally turned back. It was my impression that Professor MacMillan would command it, but Commander Peary sent the Doctor back in charge, with the two boys Arco and Wesharkoupsi. A few hours before the turning back of Dr. Goodsell, an Esquimo courier from Professor Marvin's detachment had overtaken us, with the welcome news that both Borup and Marvin, with complete loads, were immediately in our rear, safe across the lead that had so long delayed us. I was given instructions to govern my conduct for the following five marches and I was told to be ready to start right after breakfast.

Dr. Goodsell came to me, congratulated me and, with the best wishes for success, bade me good-by. He was loath to go back, but he returned to the ship with the hearty assurance of every one that he had done good and effective work, equal to the best efforts of the more experienced members of the party.

My boys, Ootah, Ahwatingwah, and Koolootingwah, under my command started north, to pioneer the route for five full marches, and it was with a firm resolve that I determined to cover a big mileage. We had been having extreme cold weather, as low as 59° below zero, and on the morning my party started the thermometers in the camp showed 49° below zero.

An hour's travel brought us to a small lead, which was avoided by making a detour, and about four miles beyond this lead we came up to heavy old floes, on which the snow lay deep and soft. The sledges would sink to the depth of the cross-bars. Traveling was slow, and the dogs became demons; at one time, sullen and stubborn; then wildly excited and savage; and in our handling of them I fear we became fiend-like ourselves. Frequently we would have to lift them bodily from the pits of snow, and snow-filled fissures they had fallen into, and I am now sorry to say that we did not do it gently. The dogs, feeling the additional strain, refused to make the slightest effort when spoken to or touched with the whip, and to break them of this stubbornness, and to prevent further trouble, I took the leader or king dog of one team and, in the presence of the rest of the pack, I clubbed him severely. The dogs realized what was required of them, and that I would exact it of them in spite of what they would do, and they became submissive and pulled willingly, myself and the Esquimos doing our share at the upstanders.

We got over the heavy floe-ice, to find ourselves confronted with jagged, rough ice, where we had to pickax our way. In one place we came to pressure-ridges separated by a deep gulch of very rough and uneven ice, in crossing which it took two men to manage each sledge, and another man to help pull them up on to the more even ice. We crossed several leads, mostly frozen over, and kept on going for over twelve hours. The mileage was small and, instead of elation, I felt discouragement. Two of the sledges had split their entire length and had to be repaired, and the going had been such that we could not cover any distance. We had a good long rest at the Big Lead for over six days, but at the end of this, my first day's pioneering, I was as tired out as I have ever been. It should be understood that while I was pioneering I was carrying the full-loaded sledges with about 550 pounds, while the other parties that were in the lead never carried but half of the regular load, which made our progress much slower.

March 15: Bright, clear, and I am sure as cold as the record-breaking cold of the day previous. We made an early start, with hopes high; but the first two hours' traveling was simply a repetition of the going of the day before. But after that, and to the end of the day's march, the surface of the ice over which we traveled was most remarkably smooth. The fallen snow had packed solid into the areas of rough ice and on the edges of the large floes. The dogs, with tails up and heads out, stamped off mile after mile in rapid succession, and when we camped I conservatively made the estimate fifteen miles. It has to be good going to make such a distance with loaded sledges, but we made it and I was satisfied.

March 16: We started going over ice conditions similar to the good part of the day before, but our hopes were soon shattered when the ice changed completely and, from being stationary, a distinct motion become observable. The movement of the ice increased, and the rumbling and roaring, as it raftered, was deafening. A dense fog, the sure indication of open water, overhung us, and in due time we came to the open lead, over which small broken floes were scattered, interspersed with thin young ice. These floes were hardly thick enough to hold a dog safely, but, there being no other way, we were obliged to cross on them. We set out with jaws squared by anxiety. A false step by any one would mean the end. With the utmost care, the sledges were placed on the most solid floes, and, with Ootah, the most experienced, in the lead, we followed in single file. Once started, there was no stopping; but push on with the utmost care and even pressure. You know that we got across, but there were instants during the crossing when I had my strongest doubts. After crossing the lead, the ice condition became horrible. Almost at the same time, three of the sledges broke, one sledge being completely smashed to pieces. We were forced to camp and start to work making two whole sledges from the wreckage of the three broken ones.

We had barely completed this work when the Commander, the Captain, Marvin, Borup, and Esquimos came in. I was glad to see them all again, especially the smiling face of George Borup, whom I had not seen since the day he left Cape Columbia.

We learned that MacMillan had been sent back to the ship on the 15th, that the party had been delayed on the second day's march by a new lead, which widened so rapidly and to such an extent that it was feared to be the twin sister of the Big Lead farther back.

March 17: The whole party, with the exception of Professor Marvin and his detachment, remained in camp. Marvin was sent ahead to plot a route for the next marches of the column, and the party in camp busied itself in the general work of repairing sledges and equipment.

The morning of the 18th found the main column ready to start, and start it did, in spite of the dreary outlook due to the condition of the weather and of the ice. Thermometer 40° below zero, and the loose ice to our right and in front distinctly in motion, but fortunately moving to the northward. A heavy wind of the force of a gale was at our backs, and for the first three miles our progress was slow. The hummocks of ice in wild disarrangement, and so difficult to cross that repeatedly the sledges were overturned; and one sledge was broken so badly that a halt had to be made to repair it. While repairing the sledge, our midday lunch of crackers was eaten. The dogs were not fed anything, experience having taught us that dogs will work better with hope for a reward in the future than when it is past.

All that day the air was thick with haze and frost and we felt the cold even more than when the temperature was lower with the air clear. The wind would find the tiniest opening in our clothing and pierce us with the force of driving needles. Our hoods froze to our growing beards and when we halted we had to break away the ice that had been formed by the congealing of our breaths and from the moisture of perspiration exhaled by our bodies. When we finally camped and built our igloos, it was not with any degree of comfort that we lay down to rest. Actually it was more comfortable to keep on the march, and when we did rest it was fatigue that compelled.

CHAPTER XIII

The Supporting-Parties Begin to Turn Back

MARCH 19: WE LEFT CAMP in a haze of bitter cold; the ice conditions about the same as the previous day; high rafters, huge and jagged; and we pickaxed the way continuously. By noontime, we found ourselves alongside of a lead covered by a film of young ice. We forced the dogs and they took it on the run, the ice undulating beneath them, the same as it does when little wanton boys play at *tickley benders,* often with serious results, on the newly formed ice on ponds and brooks down in civilization. Our *tickley benders* were not done in the spirit of play, but on account of urgent necessity, and as it was I nearly suffered a serious loss of precious possessions.

One of the sledges, driven by Ahwatingwah, broke through the ice and its load, which consisted of my extra equipment, such as kamiks, mittens, etc., was thoroughly soaked. Luckily for the boy, he was at the side of the sledge and escaped a ducking. Foolishly I rushed over, but, quickly realizing my danger, I slowed down, and with the utmost care he fished out the sledge, and the dogs, shaking as with palsy, were gently urged on. Walking wide, like the polar bear, we crept after, and without further incident reached the opposite side of the lead. My team had reached there before me and, with human intelligence, the dogs had dragged the sledges to a place of safety and were sitting on their haunches, with ears cocked forward, watching us in our precarious predicament. They seemed to rejoice at our deliverance, and as I went among them and untangled their traces I could not forbear giving each one an affectionate pat on the head.

For the next five hours our trail lay over heavy pressure ridges, in some places sixty feet high. We had to make a trail over the mountains of ice and then come back for the sledges. A difficult climb began. Pushing from our very toes, straining every muscle, urging the dogs with voice and whip, we guided the sledges. On several occasions the dogs gave it up, standing still in their tracks, and we had to hold the sledges with the strength of our bones and muscles to prevent them from sliding backwards. When we had regained our equilibrium the dogs were again started, and in this way we gained the tops of the pressure-ridges.

Going down on the opposite side was more nerve-racking. On the descent of one ridge, in spite of the experienced care of Ootah, the sledge bounded away from him, and at a declivity of thirty feet was completely wrecked. The frightened dogs dashed wildly in every direction to escape the falling sledge, and as quickly as possible we slid down the steep incline, at the same time guiding the dogs attached to the two remaining sledges. We rushed over, my two boys and I, to the spot where the poor dogs stood trembling with fright. We released them from the tangle they were in, and, with kind words and pats of the hand on their heads, quieted them. For over an hour we struggled with the broken pieces of the wreck and finally lashed them together with strips of *oog-sook* (seal-hide). We said nothing to the Commander when he caught up with us, but his quick eye took in at a glance the experience we had been through. The repairs having been completed, we again started. Before us stretched a heavy, old floe, giving us good going until we reached the lead, when the order was given to camp. We built our igloos, and boiled the tea and had what we called supper.

Commander Peary called me over to his igloo and gave me my orders: first; that I should at once select the best dogs of the three teams, as the ones disqualified by me would on the following morning be sent back to the ship, in care of the third supporting-party, which was to turn back. Secondly; that I should rearrange the loads on the remainder of the sledges, there now being ten in number. It was eight P.M. when I began work and two the following morning when I had finished.

March 20: During the night, the Commander had a long talk with Borup, and in the morning my good friend, in command of the third supporting-party, bade us all good-by and took his detachment back to land and headquarters. There were three Esquimos and seventeen dogs in his party. A fine and plucky young man, whose cheerful manner and ready willingness had made him a prime favorite; and he had done his work like an old campaigner.

At the time of Borup's turning southward, Captain Bartlett, with two Esquimos, started out to the north to make trail. He was to act as pioneer. At ten-thirty A.M., I, with two Esquimos, followed; leaving at the igloos the Commander and Professor Marvin, with four Esquimos.

The system of our marches from now on was that the first party, or pioneers, which consisted of Captain Bartlett, myself, and our Esquimos, should be trail-making, while the second party, consisting of Commander Peary and Marvin, with their Esquimos, should be sleeping; and while the first party was sleeping, the second should be traveling over the trail previously made. The sun was above the horizon the whole twenty-four hours of the day, and accordingly there was no darkness. Either the first or second party was always traveling, and progress was hourly made.

March 21: Captain Bartlett got away early, leaving me in camp to await the arrival of Commander Peary and Marvin, with their party; and it was eight A.M. when they arrived. Commander Peary instructed me to the effect that, when I overtook the Captain, I should tell him to make as much speed as possible.

The going was, for the first hour, over rough, raftered ice. Great care and caution had to be observed, but after that we reached a stretch of undulated, level ice, extending easily fifteen miles; and the exhilarating effect made our spirits rise. The snow-covering was soft, but with the help of our snow-shoes we paced off the miles, and at noon we caught up with the Captain and his boys. Together we traveled on, and at the end of an hour's going we halted for our noon-meal, consisting of a can of tea and three biscuits per man, the dogs doing the hungry looking on, as dogs have done and do and will do forever. As we sat and ate, we joshed each other, and the Esquimo boys joined in the good-natured railery.

The meal did not detain us long, and soon we were pushing on again as quickly as possible over the level ice, fearing that if we delayed the condition of the ice would change, for changes come suddenly, and frequently without warning. At nine P.M. we camped, the Captain having been on the go for fifteen hours, and I for thirteen; and we estimated that we had a good fourteen miles to our credit.

March 22 was the finest day we had, and it was a day of unusual clearness and calm; practically no wind and a cloudless sky. The fields of ice and snow sparkled and glistened and the daylight lasted for the full twenty-four hours. It was six A.M. when Egingwah, the Commander's Esquimo courier, reached our camp, with the note of command and encouragement; and immediately the Captain and I left camp.

Stretching to the northward was a brilliantly illuminated, level, and slightly drifted snow-plain, our imperial highway, presenting a spectacle grand and sublime; and we were truly grateful and inwardly prayed that this condition would last indefinitely. Without incident or accident, we marched on for fifteen hours, pacing off mile after mile in our steady northing, and at nine P.M. we halted. It was then we realized how utterly fatigued and exhausted we were. It took us over an hour and a half to build our igloos. We had a hard time finding suitable snow conditions for building them, and the weather was frightfully cold. The evening meal of pemmican-stew and tea was prepared, the dogs were fed, and we turned in.

March 23: Our sleep-banked eyes were opened by the excitement caused by the arrival of Marvin and his division. He reported the same good going that we had had the day before, and also that he had taken an elevation of the sun and computed his latitude as 85° 46′ north. We turned the igloos over to Marvin and his Esquimos, who were to await the arrival of the Commander, and Captain Bartlett and myself got our parties under way.

Conditions are never similar, no two days are the same; and our going this day was nothing like the paradise of the day before. At a little distance from the igloos we encountered high masses of heavily rubbled, old ice. The making of a trail through these masses of ice caused us to use our pickaxes continuously. It was backing and filling all of the time. First we would reconnoiter, then we would hew our way and make the trail, then we would go back and, getting in the traces, help the dogs pull the sledges, which were still heavily loaded. This operation was repeated practically all the day of March 23, except for the last hour of traveling, when we zigzagged to the eastward, where the ice appeared less formidable, consisting of small floes with rubble ice between and a heavy, old floe beyond. There we camped. The latitude was 85° 46′ north.

The course from the land to the Pole was not direct and due north, for we followed the lines of least resistance, and frequently found ourselves going due east or west, in order to detour around pressure-ridges, floebergs, and leads.

March 24: Commander Peary reached camp shortly after six A.M., and after a few brief instructions, we started out. The going not as heavy as the day previous; but the sky overcast, and a heavy drift on the surface made it decidedly unpleasant for the dogs. For the first six hours the going was over rough, jagged ice, covered with deep, soft snow; for the rest of the day it improved. We encountered comparatively level ice, with a few hummocks, and in places covered with deep snow. We camped at eight P.M., beside a very heavy pressure-ridge as long as a city street and as high as the houses along the street.

March 25: Turned out at four-thirty A.M., to find a steadily falling snow storm upon us. We breakfasted, and fifteen minutes later we were once more at work making trail. Our burly neighbor, the pressure-ridge, in whose lee we had spent the night, did not make an insuperable obstacle, and in the course of an hour we had made a trail across it, and returned to the igloo for the sledges. We found that the main column had reached camp, and after greetings had been given, Commander Peary called me aside and gave me my orders; to take the trail at once, to speed it up to the best of my ability and cover as much distance as possible; for he intended that I should remain at the igloo the following day to sort out the best dogs and rearrange the loads, as Marvin was to turn back with the fourth supporting-party. My heart stopped palpitating, I breathed easier, and my mind was relieved. It was not my turn yet, I was to continue onward and there only remained one person between me and the Pole—the Captain. We knew Commander Peary's general plan: that, at the end of certain periods, certain parties would turn south to the land and the ship; but we did not know who would comprise or command those parties and, until I had the Commander's word, I feared that I would be the next after Borup. At the same time, I did not see how Marvin could travel much longer, as his feet were very badly frozen.

Obedient to the Commander's orders, the Captain, I, and our Esquimos, left camp with loaded sledges and trudged over the newly made trail, coming to rough ice which stretched for a distance of five miles, and kept us hard at back-straining, shoulder-wrenching work for several hours. The rest of the day's march was over level, unbroken, young ice; and the distance covered was considerable.

March 26: The Commander and party reached the igloo at ten-forty-five A.M. Captain Bartlett had taken to the trail at six A.M., and was now miles to the northward, out of sight. I immediately started to work on the task assigned me by the Commander, assorting the dogs first, so that the different king dogs could fight it out and adjust themselves to new conditions while I was rearranging the loads.

At twelve, noon, Professor Marvin took his final sight, and after figuring it out told me that he made it 86° 38′ north.

The work of readjusting the loads kept me busy until seven P.M. While doing this work I came across my Bible that I had neglected so long, and that night, before going to sleep, I read the twenty-third psalm, and the fifth chapter of St. Matthew.

March 27: I was to take the trail at six A.M., but before starting I went over to Marvin's igloo to bid him good-by. In his quiet, earnest manner, he advised me to keep on, and hoped for our success; he congratulated me and we gave each other the strong, fraternal grip of our honored fraternity and we confidently expected to see each other again at the ship. My good, kind friend was never again to see us, or talk with us. It is sad to write this. He went back to his death, drowned in the cold, black water of the Big Lead. In unmarked, unmarbled grave, he sleeps his last, long sleep.

CHAPTER XIV

Bartlett's Farthest North—His Quiet Good-by

LEAVING THE COMMANDER and Marvin at the igloos, my party took up the Captain's trail northward. It was expected that Peary would follow in an hour and that at the same time Marvin would start his return march. After a few minutes' going, we came to young ice of this season, broken up and frozen solid, not difficult to negotiate, but requiring constant pulling; leaving this, we came to an open lead which caused us to make a detour to the westward for four miles. We crossed on ice so thin that one of the sledge-runners broke through, and a little beyond one of the dogs fell in so completely that it was a precarious effort to rescue him; but we made it and, dog-like, he shook the water out of his fur and a little later, when his fur froze, I gave him a thorough beating; not for falling in the water, but in order to loosen the ice-particles, so that he could shake them off. Poor brute, it was no use, and in a short while he commenced to develop symptoms of the dread piblokto, so in mercy he was killed. One of the Esquimo boys did the killing.

Dangerous as the crossing was, it was the only place possible, and we succeeded far better than we had anticipated. Beyond the lead we came to an old floe and, beyond that, young ice of one season's formation, similar to that which had been encountered earlier in the day. Before us lay a heavy, old floe, covered with soft, deep snow in which we sank continually; but it was only five P.M. when we reached the Captain's igloo. Anticipating the arrival of the Commander, we built another igloo, and about an hour and a half later the Commander and his party came in.

March 28: Exactly 40° below zero when we pushed the sledges up to the curled-up dogs and started them off over rough ice covered with deep soft snow. It was like walking in loose granulated sugar. Indeed I might compare the snow of the Arctic to the granules of sugar, without their saccharine sweetness, but with freezing cold instead; you can not make snowballs of it, for it is too thoroughly congealed, and when it is packed by the wind it is almost as solid as ice. It is from the packed snow that the blocks used to form the igloo-walls are cut.

At the end of four hours, we came to the igloo where the Captain and his boys were sleeping the sleep of utter exhaustion. In order not to interrupt the Captain's rest, we built another igloo and unloaded his sledge, and distributed the greater part of the load among the sledges of the party. The Captain, on awakening, told us that the journey we had completed on that day had been made by him under the most trying conditions, and that it had taken him fourteen hours to do it. We were able to make better time because we had his trail to follow, and, therefore, the necessity of finding the easiest way was avoided. That was the object of the scout or pioneer party and Captain Bartlett had done practically all of it up to the time he turned back at 87° 48′ north.

March 29: You have undoubtedly taken into consideration the pangs of hunger and of cold that you know assailed us, going Pole-ward; but have you ever considered that we were thirsty for water to drink or hungry for fat? To eat snow to quench our thirsts would have been the height of folly, and as well as being thirsty, we were continuously assailed by the pangs of a hunger that called for the fat, good, rich, oily, juicy fat that our systems craved and demanded.

Had we succumbed to the temptations of thirst and eaten the snow, we would not be able to tell the tale of the conquest of the Pole; for the result of eating snow is death. True, the dogs licked up enough moisture to quench their thirsts, but we were not made of such stern stuff as they. Snow would have reduced our temperatures and we would quickly have fallen by the way. We had to wait until camp was made and the fire of alcohol started before we had a chance, and it was with hot tea that we quenched our thirsts. The hunger for fat was not appeased; a dog or two was killed, but his carcass went to the Esquimos and the entrails were fed to the rest of the pack. We ate no dogs on this trip, for various reasons, mainly, that the eating of dog is only a last resort, and we had plenty of food, and raw dog is flavorless and very tough. The killing of a dog is such a horrible matter that I will not describe it, and it is permitted only when all other exigencies have been exhausted. An Esquimo does not permit one drop of blood to escape.

The morning of the 29th of March 1909, a heavy and dense fog of frost spicules overhung the camp. At four A.M., the Captain left camp to make as far a northing as possible. I with my Esquimos followed later. On our way we passed over very rough ice alternating with small floes, young ice of a few months' duration, and one old floe. We were now beside a lead of over three hundred feet in width, which we were unable to cross at that time because the ice was running steadily, though to the northward. Following the trail of the Captain, which carried us a little to the westward of the lead, within one hundred feet of the Captain's igloo, the order to camp was given, as going forward was impossible. The whole party was together farther north than had ever been made by any other human beings, and in perfectly good condition; but the time was quickly coming when the little party would have to be made smaller and some part of it sent back. We were too fatigued to argue the question.

We turned in for a rest and sleep, but soon turned out again in pandemonium incomprehensible; the ice moving in all directions, our igloos wrecked, and every instant our very lives in danger. With eyes dazed by sleep, we tried to guide the terror-stricken dogs and push the sledges to safety, but rapidly we saw the party being separated and the black water begin to appear amid the roar of the breaking ice floes.

To the westward of our igloo stood the Captain's igloo, on an island of ice, which revolved, while swiftly drifting to the eastward. On one occasion the floe happened to strike the main floe. The Captain, intently watching his opportunity, quickly crossed with his Esquimos. He had scarcely set foot on the opposite floe when the floe on which he had been previously isolated swung off, and rapidly disappeared.

Once more the parties were together. Thoroughly exhausted, we turned in and fell asleep, myself and the Esquimos too dumb for utterance, and Commander Peary and Bartlett too full of the realization of our escape to have much to say.

The dogs were in very good condition, taking everything into consideration.

When we woke up it was the morning of another day, March 30, and we found open water all about us. We could not go on until either the lead had frozen or until it had raftered shut. Temperature 35° below zero, and the weather clear and calm with no visible motion of the ice. We spent the day industriously in camp, mending foot-gear, harness, clothing, and looking after the dogs and their traces. This was work enough, especially untangling the traces of the bewildered dogs. The traces, snarled and entangled, besides being frozen to the consistency of wire, gave us the hardest work; and, owing to the activity of the dogs in leaping and bounding over each other, we had the most *unideal* conditions possible to contend with, and we were handicapped by having to use mitted instead of ungloved fingers to untangle the snarls of knots. Unlike Alexander the Great, we dared not cut the "Gordian Knots," but we did get them untangled.

About five o'clock in the afternoon, the temperature had fallen to 43° below zero, and at the same time the ice began to move again. Owing to the attraction of the moon, the mighty flanks of the earth were being drawn by her invisible force, and were commencing again to crack and be rent asunder.

We loaded up hurriedly and all three parties left the camp and crossed over the place where recently had been the open lead, and beyond for more than five miles, until we reached the heavier and solid ice of the large floes. Northward our way led, and we kept on in that direction accordingly, at times crossing young ice so thin that the motion of the sledges would cause the ice to undulate. Over old floes of the blue, hummocky kind, on which the snow had fallen and become packed solid, the rest of this day's journey was completed. We staggered into camp like drunken men, and built our igloos by force of habit rather than with the intelligence of human beings.

It was continuously daylight, but such a light as never was on land or sea.

The next day was April 1, and the Farthest North of Bartlett. I knew at this time that he was to go back, and that I was to continue, so I had no misgivings and neither had he. He was ready and anxious to take the back-trail. His five marches were up and he was glad of it, and he was told that in the morning he must turn back and knit the trail together, so that the main column could return over a beaten path.

Before going to sleep, Peary and he (Captain Bartlett) had figured out the reckoning of the distance, and, to insure the Captain's making at least 88° north, Peary let him have another go, for a short distance northward, and at noon on the day of his return, the observations showed that Captain Bartlett had made 87° 47′ North Latitude, or practically 88° north. "Why, Peary," he said, "it is just like every day," and so it was, with this exception, like every day in the Arctic, but with all of every day's chances and hazards. The lion-like month of March had passed. Captain Bartlett bade us all farewell. He turned back from the Farthest North that had ever been reached by any one, to insure the safe return of him who was to go to a still Farther North, the very top of the world, the Pole itself.

While waiting for Bartlett to return from his forced march, the main party had been at work, assorting dogs (by this time without much trouble, as only one was found utterly unfit to make progress), and rearranging loads, for the Captain had almost three hundred miles of sea-ice to negotiate before he would reach *terra firma,* and he had to have his food-supply arranged so that it would carry him to the land and back to the ship, and dogs in good enough condition to pull the loads, as well as enough sledges to bear his equipment. When he did come back to our camp, before the parting, he was perfectly satisfied, and with the same old confidence he swept his little party together and at three P.M., with a cheery "Good-by! Good Luck!" he was off. His Esquimo boys, attempting in English, too, gave us their "Good-bys." The least emotional of all of our partings; and this brave man, who had borne the brunt of all of the hardships, like the true-blue, dead-game, unconquerable hero that he was, set out to do the work that was left for him to do; to knit the broken strands of our upward trail together, so that we who were at his rear could follow in safety.

I have never heard the story of the return of Captain Bartlett in detail; his Esquimo boys were incapable of telling it, and Captain Bartlett is altogether too modest.

CHAPTER XV

The Pole!

CAPTAIN BARTLETT AND HIS two boys had commenced their return journey, and the main column, depleted to its final strength, started northward. We were six: Peary, the commander, the Esquimos, Ootah, Egingwah, Seegloo and Ooqueah, and myself.

Day and night were the same. My thoughts were on the going and getting forward, and on nothing else. The wind was from the southeast, and seemed to push us on, and the sun was at our backs, a ball of livid fire, rolling his way above the horizon in never-ending day.

The Captain had gone, Commander Peary and I were alone (save for the four Esquimos), the same as we had been so often in the past years, and as we looked at each other we realized our position and we knew without speaking that the time had come for us to demonstrate that we were the men who, it had been ordained, should unlock the door which held the mystery of the Arctic. Without an instant's hesitation, the order to push on was given, and we started off in the trail made by the Captain to cover the Farthest North he had made and to push on over one hundred and thirty miles to our final destination.

The Captain had had rough going, but, owing to the fact that his trail was our track for a short time, and that we came to good going shortly after leaving his turning point, we made excellent distance without any trouble, and only stopped when we came to a lead barely frozen over, a full twenty-five miles beyond. We camped and waited for the strong southeast wind to force the sides of the lead together. The Esquimos had eaten a meal of stewed dog, cooked over a fire of wood from a discarded sledge, and, owing to their wonderful powers of recuperation, were in good condition; Commander Peary and myself, rested and invigorated by our thirty hours in the last camp, waiting for the return and departure of Captain Bartlett, were also in fine fettle, and accordingly the accomplishment of twenty-five miles of northward progress was not exceptional. With my proven ability in gauging distances, Commander Peary was ready to take the reckoning as I made it and he did not resort to solar observations until we were within a hand's grasp of the Pole.

The memory of those last five marches, from the Farthest North of Captain Bartlett to the arrival of our party at the Pole, is a memory of toil, fatigue, and exhaustion, but we were urged on and encouraged by our relentless commander, who was himself being scourged by the final lashings of the dominating influence that had controlled his life. From the land to 87° 48′ north, Commander Peary had had the best of the going, for he had brought up the rear and had utilized the trail made by the preceding parties, and thus he had kept himself in the best of condition for the time when he made the spurt that brought him to the end of the race. From 87° 48′ north, he kept in the lead and did his work in such a way as to convince me that he was still as good a man as he had ever been. We marched and marched, falling down in our tracks repeatedly, until it was impossible to go on. We were forced to camp, in spite of the impatience of the Commander, who found himself unable to rest, and who only waited long enough for us to relax into sound sleep, when he would wake us up and start us off again. I do not believe that he slept for one hour from April 2 until after he had loaded us up and ordered us to go back over our old trail, and I often think that from the instant when the order to return was given until the land was again sighted, he was in a continual daze.

Onward we forced our weary way. Commander Peary took his sights from the time our chronometer-watches gave, and I, knowing that we had kept on going in practically a straight line, was sure that we had more than covered the necessary distance to insure our arrival at the top of the earth.

It was during the march of the 3rd of April that I endured an instant of hideous horror. We were crossing a lane of moving ice. Commander Peary was in the lead setting the pace, and a half hour later the four boys and myself followed in single file. They had all gone before, and I was standing and pushing at the upstanders of my sledge, when the block of ice I was using as a support slipped from underneath my feet, and before I knew it the sledge was out of my grasp, and I was floundering in the water of the lead. I did the best I could. I tore my hood from off my head and struggled frantically. My hands were gloved and I could not take hold of the ice, but before I could give the "Grand Hailing Sigh of Distress," faithful old Ootah had grabbed me by the nape of the neck, the same as he would have grabbed a dog, and with one hand he pulled me out of the water, and with the other hurried the team across.

He had saved my life, but I did not tell him so, for such occurrences are taken as part of the day's work, and the sledge he safe-guarded was of much more importance, for it held, as part of its load, the Commander's sextant, the mercury, and the coils of piano-wire that were the essential portion of the scientific part of the expedition. My kamiks (boots of sealskin) were stripped off, and the congealed water was beaten out of my bearskin trousers, and with a dry pair of kamiks, we hurried on to overtake the column. When we caught up, we found the boys gathered around the Commander, doing their best to relieve him of his discomfort, for he had fallen into the water also, and while he was not complaining, I was sure that his bath had not been any more voluntary than mine had been.

When we halted on April 6, 1909, and started to build the igloos, the dogs and sledges having been secured, I noticed Commander Peary at work unloading his sledge and unpacking several bundles of equipment. He pulled out from under his *kooletah* (thick, fur outer-garment) a small folded package and unfolded it. I recognized his old silk flag, and realized that this was to be a camp of importance. Our different camps had been known as Camp Number One, Number Two, etc., but after the turning back of Captain Bartlett, the camps had been given names such as Camp Nansen, Camp Cagni, etc., and I asked what the name of this camp was to be — "Camp Peary"? "This, my boy, is to be Camp Morris K. Jesup, the last and most northerly camp on the earth." He fastened the flag to a staff and planted it firmly on the top of his igloo. For a few minutes it hung limp and lifeless in the dead calm of the haze, and then a slight breeze, increasing in strength, caused the folds to straighten out, and soon it was rippling out in sparkling color. The Stars and Stripes were "nailed to the Pole."

A thrill of patriotism ran through me and I raised my voice to cheer the starry emblem of my native land. The Esquimos gathered around and, taking the time from Commander Peary, three hearty cheers rang out on the still, frosty air, our dumb dogs looking on in puzzled surprise. As prospects for getting a sight of the sun were not good, we turned in and slept, leaving the flag proudly floating above us.

This was a thin silk flag that Commander Peary had carried on all of his Arctic journeys, and he had always flown it at his last camps. It was as glorious and as inspiring a banner as any battle-scarred, blood-stained standard of the world — and this badge of honor and courage was also blood-stained and battle-scarred, for at several places there were blank squares marking the spots where pieces had been cut out at each of the "Farthests" of its brave bearer, and left with the records in the cairns, as mute but eloquent witnesses of his achievements. At the North Pole a diagonal strip running from the upper left to the lower right corner was cut and this precious strip, together with a brief record, was placed in an empty tin, sealed up and buried in the ice, as a record for all time.

Commander Peary also had another American flag, sewn on a white ground, and it was the emblem of the "Daughters of the Revolution Peace Society"; he also had and flew the emblem of the Navy League, and the emblems of a couple of college fraternities of which he was a member.

It was about ten or ten-thirty A.M., on the 7th of April 1909, that the Commander gave the order to build a snow-shield to protect him from the flying drift of the surface-snow. I knew that he was about to take an observation, and while we worked I was nervously apprehensive, for I felt that the end of our journey had come. When we handed him the pan of mercury the hour was within a very few minutes of noon. Laying flat on his stomach, he took the elevation and made the notes on a piece of tissue-paper at his head. With sun-blinded eyes, he snapped shut the *vernier* (a graduated scale that subdivides the smallest divisions on the sector of the circular scale of the sextant) and with the resolute squaring of his jaws, I was sure that he was satisfied, and I was confident that the journey had ended. Feeling that the time had come, I ungloved my right hand and went forward to congratulate him on the success of our eighteen years of effort, but a gust of wind blew something into his eye, or else the burning pain caused by his prolonged look at the reflection of the limb of the sun forced him to turn aside; and with both hands covering his eyes, he gave us orders to not let him sleep for more than four hours, for six hours later he purposed to take another sight about four miles beyond, and that he wanted at least two hours to make the trip and get everything in readiness.

I unloaded a sledge, and reloaded it with a couple of skins, the instruments, and a cooker with enough alcohol and food for one meal for three, and then I turned in to the igloo where my boys were already sound asleep. The thermometer registered 29° below zero. I fell into a dreamless sleep and slept for about a minute, so I thought, when I was awakened by the clatter and noise made by the return of Peary and his boys.

The Commander gave the word, "We will plant the Stars and Stripes — *at the North Pole!*" and it was done; on the peak of a huge paleocrystic floeberg the glorious banner was unfurled to the breeze, and as it snapped and crackled with the wind, I felt a savage joy and exultation. Another world's accomplishment was done and finished, and as in the past, from the beginning of history, wherever the world's work was done by a white man, he had been accompanied by a colored man. From the building of the pyramids and the journey to the Cross, to the discovery of the new world and the discovery of the North Pole, the Negro had been the faithful and constant companion of the Caucasian, and I felt all that it was possible for me to feel, that it was I, a lowly member of my race, who had been chosen by fate to represent it, at this, almost the last of the world's great *work*.

The four Esquimos who stood with Commander Peary at the North Pole, were the brothers, Ootah and Egingwah, the old campaigner, Seegloo, and the sturdy, boyish Ooqueah. Four devoted companions, blindly confident in the leader, they worked only that he might succeed and for the promise of reward that had been made before they had left the ship, which promise they were sure would be kept. Together with the faithful dogs, these men had insured the success of the master. They had all the characteristics of the dogs, including the dogs' fidelity. Within their breasts lingered the same infatuations that Commander Peary seemed to inspire in all who were with him, and though frequently complaining and constantly requiring to be urged to do their utmost, they worked faithfully and willingly. Ootah, of my party, was the oldest, a married man, of about thirty-four years, and regarded as the best all around member of the tribe, a great hunter, a kind father, and a good provider. Owing to his strong character and the fact that he was more easily managed by me than by any of the others, he had been a member of my party from the time we left the ship. Without exaggeration, I can say that we had both saved each other's lives more than once, but it had all gone in as part of the day's work, and neither of us dwelt on our obligations to the other.

My other boy, Ooqueah, was a young man of about nineteen or twenty, very sturdy and stocky of build, and with an open, honest countenance, a smile that was "child-like and bland," and a character that *was* child-like and bland. It was alleged that the efforts of young Ooqueah were spurred on by the shafts of love, and that it was in the hopes of winning the hand of the demure Miss Anadore, the charming daughter of Ikwah, the first Esquimo of Commander Peary's acquaintance, that he worked so valiantly. His efforts were of an ardent character, but it was not due to the ardor of love, as far as I could see, but to his desire to please and his anxiety to win the promised rewards that would raise him to the grade of a millionaire, according to Esquimo standards.

Commander Peary's boy, Egingwah, was the brother of my boy Ootah, also married and of good report in his community, and it was he who drove the Morris K. Jesup sledge.

If there was any sentiment among the Esquimos in regard to the success of the venture, Ootah and Seegloo by their unswerving loyalty and fidelity expressed it. They had been members of the "Farthest North party" in 1906, the party that was almost lost beyond and in the Big Lead, and only reached the land again in a state of almost complete collapse. They were the ones who, on bidding Commander Peary farewell in 1906, when he was returning, a saddened and discouraged man, told him to be of good cheer and that when he came back again Ootah and Seegloo would go along, and stay until Commander Peary had succeeded, and they did. The cowardice of their fellow Esquimos at the Big Lead on this journey did not in the least demoralize them, and when they were absolutely alone on the trail, with every chance to turn back and return to comfort, wife, and family, they remained steadfast and true, and ever northward guided their sledges.

CHAPTER XVI

The Fast Trek Back to Land

THE LONG TRAIL WAS FINISHED, the work was done, and there was only left for us to return and tell the tale of the doing. Reaction had set in, and it was with quavering voice that Commander Peary gave the order to break camp. Already the strain of the hard upward-journey was beginning to tell, and after the first two marches back, he was practically a dead weight, but do not think that we could have gotten back without him, for it was due to the fact that he was with us, and that we could depend upon him to direct and order us, that we were able to keep up the break-neck pace that enabled us to cover three of our upward marches on one of our return marches, and we never forgot that he was still the heart and head of the party.

It was broad daylight and getting brighter, and accordingly I knew little fear, though I did think of the ghosts of other parties, flitting in spectral form over the ice-clad wastes, especially of that small detachment of the Italian expedition of the Duke D'Abruzzi, of which to this day neither track, trace, nor remembrance has ever been found. We crossed lead after lead, sometimes like a bareback rider in the circus, balancing on cake after cake of ice, but good fortune was with us all of the way, and it was not until the land of recognizable character had been lifted that we lost the trail, and with the land in sight as an incentive, it was no trouble for us to gain the talus of the shore ice and find the trail again.

When we "hit the beach for fair" it was early in the morning of April 23, 1909, nearly seventeen days since we had left the Pole, but such a seventeen days of haste, toil, and misery as cannot be comprehended by the mind. We who experienced it, Commander Peary, the Esquimos, and myself, look back to it as to a horrid nightmare, and to describe it is impossible for me.

Commander Peary had taken the North Pole by conquest, in the face of almost insuperable natural difficulties, by the tremendous fighting-power of himself. The winning of the North Pole was a fight with nature; the way to the Pole that had been covered and retraced by Commander Peary lay across the ever moving and drifting ice of the Arctic Ocean. For more than a hundred miles from Cape Columbia it was piled in heavy pressure-ridges, ridge after ridge, some more than a hundred feet in height. In addition, open lanes of water held the parties back until the leads froze up again, and continually the steady drift of the ice carried us back on the course we had come, but due to his deathless ambition to know and to do, he had conquered. He had added to the sum of Earth's knowledge, and proven that the mind of man is boundless in its desire.

The long quest for the North Pole is over and the awful space that separated man from the *Ultima Thule* has been bridged. There is no more beyond; from Cape Columbia to Cape Chelyuskin, the route northward to the Pole, and southward again to the plains of Asia, is an open book and the geographical mind is at rest.

We found the abandoned igloos of Crane City and realized that Captain Bartlett had reached the land safely. The damage due to the action of the storms was not material. We made the necessary repairs, and in a few minutes tea was boiled and rations eaten, and we turned in for sleep. For practically all of the two days following, that was what we did: sleep and eat; men and dogs thoroughly exhausted; and we slept the sleep of the just, without apprehensions or misgivings. Our toboggan from the Pole was ended.

DIFFERENT FROM all other trips, we had not on this one been maddened by the pangs of hunger, but instead we felt the effects of lack of sleep, and brain- and body-fatigue. After reaching the land again, I gave a keen searching look at each member of the party, and I realized the strain they had been under. Instead of the plump, round countenances I knew so well, I saw lean, gaunt faces, seamed and wrinkled, the faces of old men, not those of boys, but in their eyes still shone the spark of resolute determination.

Commander Peary's face was lined and seamed, his beard was fully an inch in length, and his mustaches, which had been closely cropped before he left the ship, had again attained their full flowing length. His features expressed fatigue, but the heart-breaking look of sadness that had clung to him since the failure of the 1906 expedition, had vanished. From his steel-gray eyes flashed forth the light of glorious victory, and though he always carried himself proudly, there had come about him an air of erect assurance that was exhilarating.

When I reached the ship again and gazed into my little mirror, it was the pinched and wrinkled visage of an old man that peered out at me, but the eyes still twinkled and life was still entrancing. This wizening of our features was due to the strain of travel and lack of sleep; we had enough to eat, and I have only mentioned it to help impress the fact that the journey to the Pole and back is not to be regarded as a pleasure outing, and our so-called jaunt was by no means a cake-walk.

CHAPTER XVII

Safe on the Roosevelt*—Poor Marvin*

If you will remember, the journey from Cape Sheridan to Cape Columbia was with overloaded sledges in the darkness preceding the dawn of the Arctic day, mostly over rough going and up-hill, and now the tables were turned. It was broad day and down-hill with lightened sledges, so that we practically coasted the last miles from the twin peaks of Columbia to the low, slanting fore-shore of Sheridan and the *Roosevelt.* After the forty hours' rest at Cape Columbia, Commander Peary had his sledges loaded up, and with Egingwah and the best of the remaining dogs, he got away.

I was told I could remain at the camp for another twelve hours. A large and substantial cache of supplies had been dropped at Cape Columbia by various members of the expedition and when the Commander was gone, I gave the boys full permission to turn in and eat all they wanted, and I also gave the dogs all they could stuff, and it was not until all of us had gorged ourselves to repletion that I gave the order to *vamoose.* We were loaded to capacity, outward and inward, and we saw a bountiful supply still lying there, but we could not pack another ounce. It was early in the morning of April 25 when Peary started for the ship; it was about four or five hours later, about noon, when I gave the word, and Ootah, Seegloo, Ooqueah, and myself left Crane City, Cape Columbia, Grant Land, for the last time.

We overtook the Commander at Point Moss, and we traveled with him to Cape Colan, where we camped. Peary continued on to Sail Harbor, and we stayed in our comfortable camp and rested. We again caught up with the Commander at Porter Bay, where we camped for a few hours. The following morning I rearranged the sledges and left two of them at Porter Bay. It was my intention to reach the ship on this evening. We made a short stop at Black Cliff Bay and had lunch, and without further interruption we traveled on and at about eight-forty-five P.M. we sighted the *Roosevelt.*

The sighting of the ship was our first view of home, and far away as she was, our acutely developed senses of smell were regaled with the appetizing odor of hot coffee, and the pungent aroma of tobacco-smoke, wafted to us through the clear, germ-free air. The Esquimo boys, usually excited on the slightest provocation, were surprisingly stolid and merely remarked "*Oomiaksoah*" ("The ship") in quiet voices, until I, unable to control myself, burst forth with a loud "hip! hip! hurrah!" and with all that was left of my energy hurried my sledge in to the ship. We had been sighted almost as quickly as we had sighted the ship, and a party of the ship's crew came running out to meet us, and as we rushed on we were told about the safe arrival of Commander Peary, Bartlett, Borup, MacMillan, and Dr. Goodsell. Transported with elation and overjoyed to find myself once more safe among friends, I had rushed onward and as I recognized the different faces of the ship's company, I did not realize that some were missing.

Chief Wardwell was the first man to greet me, he photographed me as I was closing in on the ship, and with his strong right arm pulled me up over the side and hugged me to his bosom. "Good boy, Matt," he said; "too bad about Marvin," and then I knew that all was wrong and that it was not the time for rejoicing. I asked for Peary and I was told that he was all right. I saw Captain Bartlett and I knew that he was there; but where was Borup, where were MacMillan, Marvin, and where was Dr. Goodsell? Dr. Goodsell was right by my side, holding me up, and I realized that it was of him I was demanding to know of the others.

Reason had not left me, the bonds of sanity had not snapped, but for the time I was hysterical, and I only knew that all were well and safe excepting Marvin, who was drowned. A big mug of coffee was given to me, I drank a spoonful; a glass of spirits was handed me, I drank it all, and I was guided to my cabin, my fur clothes were taken off, and for the first time in sixty-eight days, I allowed myself to relax and I fell into a sleep.

When I awoke, I had the grandest feast imaginable set before me, and after eating, I had the most luxurious bath possible, and then some more to eat, and afterwards, some more sleep; then I shaved myself, combed my hair, and came out of my cabin and crossed over to the galley, and sat on a box and watched Charley at work. Then I thought of the dogs and went outside and found that they had been cared for. I wondered when the Commander would want to see me. All of the time the sailors and Charley and the Esquimo folks were keeping up a running fire of conversation, and I was able to gather from what they said that my dear, good friend, Professor Marvin, was indeed lost; that Peary had reached the *Roosevelt* about seven hours ahead of me; that Captain Bartlett was suffering with swollen legs and feet; that MacMillan and Borup with their own and Marvin's boys had gone to Cape Jesup; and that Pooadloonah and Panikpah had taken their families and returned to Esquimo land.

For days after I reached the *Roosevelt,* I did nothing but rest and eat. The strain was over and I had all but collapsed, but with constant eating and sleeping, I was quickly myself again. The pains and swellings of my limbs did not come as they had on all of the other returnings, and neither was Peary troubled. Captain Bartlett was the only one of the expedition that had been out on the sea-ice who felt any after effects. Every day, a few minutes after rising, he would notice that his ankle-, knee-, and hip-joints were swollen; and while the pain was not excessive, he was incapacitated for more than ten days, and he spent the most of his time in his cabin. When he came out of his cabin and did talk to me, it was only to compare notes and agree that our experiences proved that there was absolutely no question about our having discovered the Pole.

Captain Bartlett, Dr. Goodsell, Chief Wardwell, Percy—they could talk as they would; but the one ever-present thought in my mind was of Marvin, and of his death. I thought of him, and of his kindness to me; and the picture of his widowed mother, patiently waiting the return of her son, was before me all of the time. I thought of my own mother, whom I scarcely remembered, and I sincerely wished that it had been me who had been taken. When MacMillan and Borup returned, I learned all about the sad affair, from Kudlooktoo and Harrigan, and I feel that had he been with civilized companions the sad story of Marvin's death would not have to be told.

On breaking camp he had gone on, leaving the boys to load up and follow him. They were going south to the land and the ship, and there was no need for him to stay with them, and when they came up to where he had disappeared, they saw the ice newly formed about him, his head and feet beneath, and nothing showing but the fur clothing of his back and shoulders. They made no effort to rescue him, and had they succeeded in getting his body out, there is little chance that they could have kept him alive, for the temperature was far below zero, and they knew nothing about restoring life to the drowned. No blame can be laid to his childish companions.

He died alone, and he passed into the great unknown alone, bravely and honorably. He is the last of Earth's great martyrs; he is home; his work is done; he is where he longed to be; the Sailor is Home in the Sea. It is poor satisfaction to those that he left behind that his grave is the northernmost grave on the earth; but they realize that the sacrifice was not made in vain, for it was due to him that those who followed were able to keep the trail and reach the land again. The foolish boys, in accordance with Esquimo tradition, had unloaded all of Prof. Marvin's personal effects on the ice, so that his spirit should not follow them, and they hurried on back to land and to the ship, where they told their sad story.

CHAPTER XVIII

After Musk-Oxen—The Doctor's Scientific Expedition

FROM THE TIME OF MY ARRIVAL at the *Roosevelt,* for nearly three weeks, my days were spent in complete idleness. I would catch a fleeting glimpse of Commander Peary, but not once in all of that time did he speak a word to me. Then he spoke to me in the most ordinary, matter-of-fact way, and ordered me to get to work. Not a word about the North Pole or anything connected with it; simply, "There is enough wood left, and I would like to have you make a couple of sledges and mend the broken ones. I hope you are feeling all right." There was enough wood left and I made three sledges, as well as repaired those that were broken.

The Commander was still running things and he remained the commander to the last minute; nothing escaped him, and when the time came to slow-down on provisions, he gave the orders, and we had but two spare meals a day to sustain us. The whole expedition lived on travel rations from before the time we left Cape Sheridan until we had reached Sidney, N.S., and like the keen-fanged hounds, we were always ready and fit.

It was late in May when Prof. MacMillan and Mr. Borup, with their Esquimo companions, returned from Cape Jesup, where they had been doing highly important scientific work, taking soundings out on the sea-ice north of the cape as high as 84° 15′ north, and also at the cape. They had made a trip that was record-breaking; they had visited the different cairns made by Lockwood and Brainard and by Commander Peary, and they had also captured and brought into the ship a musk-ox calf; and they had most satisfactorily demonstrated their fitness as Arctic explorers, having followed the Commander's orders implicitly, and secured more than the required number of tidal-readings and soundings.

Prof. MacMillan, with Jack Barnes, a sailor, and Kudlooktoo, left for Fort Conger early in June, and continued the work of tidal-observations. They rejoined the *Roosevelt* just before she left Cape Sheridan. A little later in the month, Borup went to Clements Markham Inlet to hunt musk-oxen, and from there he went to Cape Columbia, where he erected the cairn containing the record of the last and successful expedition of the "Peary Arctic Club." The cairn was a substantial pile of rocks, surmounted by a strong oaken guide-post, with arms pointing "North 413 miles to the Pole"; "East, to Cape Morris K. Jesup, 275 miles"; "West to Cape Thomas H. Hubbard, 225 miles"; while the southern arm pointed south, but to no particular geographical spot; it was labeled "Cape Columbia." Underneath the arms of the guide-post, which had been made by Mate Gushue, was a small, glass-covered, box-like arrangement, in which was encased the record of Peary's successful journey to the Pole, and the roster of the expedition, my name included. From the cross-bars, guys of galvanized wire were stretched and secured to heavy rocks, to help sustain the monument from the fury of the storms. Borup did good work, photographed the result, and the picture of the cairn, when exhibited, proved very satisfactory to the Commander.

Dr. Goodsell with two teams, and the Esquimo men, Keshungwah and Tawchingwah, left the ship on May 27, to hunt in the Lake Hazen and Ruggles River regions. They were successful in securing thirteen musk-oxen in that neighborhood, and in Bellows Valley they shot a number of the "Peary" caribou, the species *Rangifer pearyi,* a distinct class of reindeer inhabiting that region.

On the return of Dr. Goodsell, he told of his fascinating experiences in that wonderland. Leaving the *Roosevelt,* he had turned inland at Black Cliff Bay. Past the glaciers he went with his little party, down the Bellows Valley to the Ruggles River, an actual stream of clear-running water, alive with the finest of salmon trout. Adopting the Esquimo methods, he fished for these speckled beauties with joyful success. Here he rounded up and shot the herd of musk-oxen, and here he bagged his caribou. He was in a hunter's paradise and made no haste to return, but crossed overland to Discovery Harbor and the barn-like structure of Fort Conger, the headquarters of General Greely's "Lady Franklin Bay Expedition" of 1882–1883. Professor MacMillan was on his way to Fort Conger and it was with much surprise, on arriving there, that he found that Dr. Goodsell had reached it an hour before him. It was an unexpected meeting and quite a pleasure to the Professor to find the Doctor there, ready to offer him the hospitality of the fort.

Dr. Goodsell returned to the *Roosevelt* on June 15, with a load of geological, zoological, and botanical specimens almost as heavy as the loads of meat and skins he brought in. He was an ardent scientist, and viewed nearly every situation and object from the view-point of the scientist. Nothing escaped him; a peculiar form of rock or plant, the different features of the animal life, all received his close and eager attention, and he had the faculty of imparting his knowledge to others, like the born teacher that he was. He evinced an eager interest in the Esquimos and got along famously with them.

His physical equipment was the finest; a giant in stature and strength, but withal the gentlest of men having an even, mellow disposition that never was ruffled. In the field the previous spring he had accompanied the expedition beyond the Big Lead to 84° 29′, and with the strength of his broad shoulders he had pickaxed the way.

On account of his calm, quiet manner I had hesitated to form an opinion of him at first, but you can rest assured this was a "Tenderfoot" who made good.

During this time I left the ship on short hunting trips, but I was never away from the ship for more than ten or twelve hours.

ON JULY 1 quite a lead was opened in the channel south from Cape Sheridan to Cape Rawson. The ice was slowly moving southward, and the prospects for freeing the *Roosevelt* and getting her started on her homeward way were commencing to brighten. The following day a new lead opened much nearer shore, and on July 3 the Esquimos, who had been out hunting, returned from Black Cliff Bay, without game, but with the good news that as far south as Dumb Bell Bay there stretched a lead of open water. July 4, a new lead opened very close to the *Roosevelt.* The spring tides, with a strong southerly wind, had set in so very much earlier, three years before, that on July 4, 1906, the *Roosevelt* had been entirely free of ice, with clear, open water for quite a distance to the south; but this year the ship was still completely packed in the ice, and furthermore she was listed at the same angle as during the winter.

On July 5, I was detailed to help Gushue repair the more or less damaged whale-boats. The heavy and solidly packed snow of the winter had stove them in. On July 6, the anniversary of our departure from New York a year before, the greater part of the day was spent in pumping water from the top of a heavy floeberg into the ship's boilers. This work was not completed until the morning of the 7th, when the fires were started. Due to the cold, the process of getting up steam was slow work. The ice had been breaking up daily, new leads were noticed, and on this day, July 7, a new lead opened at a distance of fifty yards from the ship, and open water stretched as far south as the eye could see. All hands were put to work reloading the supplies that had been placed on shore the fall previous, for it was easy to see that the time for departure was at hand.

With the boilers in order, an attempt was made to revolve the shaft, but the propeller was too securely frozen in the ice to move, and so Captain Bartlett got out the dynamite and succeeded in freeing the bronze blades.

From the 10th of July to the 13th, a fierce storm raged, clouds of freezing spray broke over the ship, incasing her in a coat of icy mail, and the tempest forced all of the ice out of the lower end of the channel and beyond as far as the eye could see, but the *Roosevelt* still remained surrounded by ice.

The morning of the 15th, a smart breeze from the northeast was blowing, and proved of valuable assistance to us, for it caused the huge blocks of ice that were surrounding the ship to loosen their hold, and for the first time since October, 1908, the *Roosevelt* righted herself to an even keel.

By this time all of our supplies had been loaded and stored, and from the crow's-nest a stretch of open water could be seen as far as Cape Rawson. From there to Cape Union the ice was packed solid.

CHAPTER XIX

The* Roosevelt *Starts for Home—Esquimo Villages— New Dogs and New Dog Fights

IT WAS TWO-THIRTY P.M., July 17, 1909, that the *Roosevelt* pointed her bow southward and we left our winter quarters and Cape Sheridan. We were on our journey home, all hands as happy as when, a year previous, we had started on our way north, with the added satisfaction of complete success. The ship had steamed but a short distance, when, owing to the rapidly drifting ice in the channel, she had to be made fast to a floeberg. At ten-thirty P.M., the lines were loosed and a new start made. Without further incident, we reached Black Cape.

In rounding the cape the ship encountered a terrific storm, and it was with the greatest difficulty that she made any headway. The storm increased and the *Roosevelt* had to remain in the channel, surrounded by the tightly wedged floes, at the mercy of the wind. The gale continued until the evening of the 20th. The constant surging back and forth of the channel-pack, with the spring tides and the several huge masses of ice, which repeatedly crashed against the ship's sides, caused a delay of twelve days in Robeson Channel opposite Lincoln Bay. Throughout the width of the entire channel nothing could be seen but small pools of open water; two seals were seen sporting in one of these pools, and one of the Esquimos attempted to kill them, but his aim proved false.

It was not until the 25th that the ship was able to move of her own free will, small leads having opened in close proximity to her. Ootah shot a seal in one of the leads, and also harpooned a narwhal, but he did not succeed in securing either. His brother Egingwah on the following day shot two seals and harpooned a narwhal, and he secured all three of his prizes. The Esquimos had a grand feast off the skin of the narwhal, which they esteem as a great delicacy.

By the 27th the *Roosevelt* had drifted as far south as Wrangell Bay, and it was here that Slocum (Inighito) shot and secured a hood-seal, which weighed over six hundred pounds, and seal-steaks were added to the bill-of-fare.

The snow storms of the two days ceased on the 28th, and when the weather cleared sufficiently for us to ascertain our whereabouts, we were much surprised to find that we had drifted back north, opposite Lincoln Bay. During the day the wind shifted to the north. Again we drifted southward, until, just off Cape Beechey, the narrowest part of Robeson Channel, a lead stretching southward for a distance of five miles was sighted, and into this open water the ship steamed until the lead terminated in Kennedy Channel, opposite Lady Franklin Bay, where the *Roosevelt* was icebound until August 4, drifting with the pack until we were in a direct line with Cape Tyson and Bellot Isle. Three seals were captured, one a hood-seal weighing 624 pounds, being eight feet eleven inches in length; the other two were small ring-seals.

By ten A.M. of the 4th, the ice had slackened so considerably that the *Roosevelt,* under full steam, set out and rapidly worked her way down Kennedy Channel. From Crozier Island to Cape D'Urville she steamed through practically open water, but a dense fog compelled us to make fast to a large floe when almost opposite Cape Albert. It was not until one A.M. of the 7th, despite several attempts, that the ship got clear and steamed south again. Several small leads were noticed and numerous narwhals were seen, but none were captured.

At three-thirty A.M., when nearing Cape Sabine, we observed that the barometer had dropped to 29.73. A storm was coming, and every effort was made to reach Payer Harbor, but before half of the distance had been covered, the storm broke with terrific violence. The force of the gale was such that, while swinging the boats inboard, we were drenched and thoroughly chilled by the sheets of icy spray, which saturated us and instantly froze. The *Roosevelt* was blown over to starboard until the rails were submerged. To save her, she was steered into Buchanan Bay, under the lee of the cliffs, where she remained until the morning of August 8.

At an early hour, we steamed down Buchanan Bay, passed Cocked Hat Island, and a little later, Cape Sabine. At Cape Sabine was located Camp Clay, the starvation camp of the Lady Franklin Bay expedition of 1881–1883, where the five survivors of the twenty-three members of the expedition were rescued.

We entered Smith Sound. Instead of sailing on to Etah, Peary ordered the ship into Whale Sound, in order that walrus-hunting could be done, so that the Esquimos should have a plentiful supply of meat for the following winter. Three walrus were captured, when a storm sprang up with all of the suddenness of storms in this neighborhood, and the ship crossed over from Cape Alexander to Cape Chalon. Cape Chalon is a favorite resort of the Esquimos, and is known as Peter-ar-wick, on account of the walrus that are to be found here during the months of February and March.

At Nerke, just below Cape Chalon, we found the three Esquimo families of Ahsayoo, Tungwingwah, and Teddylingwah, and it was from these people we first learned of Dr. Cook's safe return from Ellesmere Land. In spite of the fact that the *Roosevelt* was overloaded with dogs, paraphernalia, and Esquimos, these three families were taken aboard.

With them were several teams of dogs. The dogs aboard ship were the survivors of the pack that had been with us all through the campaign, and a number of litters of puppies that had been whelped since the spring season. Our dogs were well acquainted with each other and dog fights were infrequent and of little interest, but the arrival of the first dog of the new party was the signal for the grandest dog fight I have ever witnessed. I feel justified in using the language of the fairy Ariel, in Shakespeare's "Tempest": "Now is Hell empty, and all the devils are here."

Backward and forward, the foredeck of the ship was a howling, snarling, biting, yelping, moving mass of fury, and it was a long round of fully ten or fifteen minutes before the two king dogs of the packs got together, and then began the battle for supremacy of the pack. It lasted for some time. It would have been useless to separate them. They would decide sooner or later, and it was better to have it over, even if one or both contestants were killed. At length the fight was ended; our old king dog, Nalegaksoah, the champion of the pack, and the laziest dog in it, was still the king. After vanquishing his opponent and receiving humble acknowledgments, King Nalegaksoah went stamping up and down before the pack and received the homage due him; the new dogs, whining and fawning and cringingly submissive, bowed down before him.

The chief pleasure of the Esquimo dogs is fighting; two dogs, the best of friends, will hair-pull and bite each other for no cause whatever, and strange dogs fight at sight; teammates fight each other on the slightest of provocations; and it seems as though sometimes the fights are held for the purpose of educating the young. When a fight is in progress, it is the usual sight to see several mother dogs, with their litters, occupying ring-side seats. I have often wondered what chance a cat would stand against an Esquimo dog.

The ship kept on, and I had turned in and slept, and on arising had found that we had reached a place called Igluduhomidy, where a single family was located. Living with this family was a very old Esquimo, Merktoshah, the oldest man in the whole tribe, and not a blood-relation to any member of it. He had crossed over from the west coast of Smith Sound the same year that Hall's expedition had wintered there, and has lived there ever since. He had been a champion polar bear and big game hunter, and though now a very old man, was still vigorous and valiant, in spite of the loss of one eye.

We stopped at Kookan, the most prosperous of the Esquimo settlements, a village of five tupiks (skin tents), housing twenty-four people, and from there we sailed to the ideal community of Karnah. Karnah is the most delightful spot on the Greenland coast. Situated on a gently southward sloping knoll are the igloos and tupiks, where I have spent many pleasant days with my Esquimo friends and learned much of the folk-lore and history. Lofty mountains, sublime in their grandeur, overtower and surround this place, and its only exposure is southward toward the sun. In winter its climate is not severe, as compared with other portions of this country, and in the perpetual daylight of summer, life here is ideal. Rivulets of clear, cold water, the beds of which are grass- and flower-covered, run down the sides of the mountains and, but for the lack of trees, the landscape is as delightful as anywhere on earth.

CHAPTER XX

Two Narrow Escapes—Arrival at Etah—
Harry Whitney—Dr. Cook's Claims

FROM KARNAH THE *Roosevelt* sailed to Itiblu, where hunting-parties secured thirty-one walrus and one seal. By the 11th of August we had reached the northern shore of Northumberland Island, where we were delayed by storm. It was shortly before noon of this day that we barely escaped another fatal calamity.

Chief Wardwell, while cleaning the rifle of Commander Peary, had the misfortune to have the piece explode while in his hands. From some unknown cause a cartridge was discharged, the projectile pierced two thick partitions of inch-and-a-half pine, and penetrated the cabin occupied by Professor MacMillan and Mr. Borup. The billet of that bullet was the shoulder and forearm of Professor MacMillan, who at the time was sound asleep in his berth. He had been lying with his arm doubled and his head resting on his hand. A half inch nearer and the bullet would have entered his brain.

As is always the case with narrow escapes, I, too, had a narrow escape, for that same bullet entered the partition on its death-dealing mission at identically the same spot where a few minutes previously *my* head had rested. Dr. Goodsell was quickly aroused, he attended Professor MacMillan, and in a short time he diagnosed the case as a "gun-shot wound." Finding no bones broken, or veins or arteries open, he soon had the Professor bandaged and comfortable.

At the time of the accident to Professor MacMillan the ship was riding at anchor, but with insufficient slack-way, so in the afternoon, when the excitement had somewhat abated, Captain Bob decided to give the ship more chain, for a storm was imminent, and he gave the order accordingly. The boatswain, in his haste to execute the order, and overestimating the amount of chain in the locker, permitted all of it to run overboard. We were in a predicament, with the storm upon us, no anchor to hold the boat, and a savage, rocky shore on which we were in danger of being wrecked. There was a small five-hundred-pound anchor with a nine-inch cable of about one hundred and fifty fathoms remaining, which was repeatedly tried, but the ship was too much for this feather-weight anchor, and dragged it at will. Commander Peary, with his usual foresight, had ordered steam as soon as the approach of the storm was noticed, and now that the steam was up, he ordered that the ship be kept head-on, and steam up and down the coast until the storm abated. The storm lasted until the night of August 13, and the best part of the following day was spent by two boat-crews of twelve men, in grappling for the lost anchor and chain, and not until they had secured it and restored it once more to its locker were they permitted to rest. With the anchor secure, walrus-hunting commenced afresh, and on the ice-floes between Hakluyt and Northumberland Islands thirty more walrus were secured.

On August 16, the *Roosevelt* steamed back to Karnah, and the Esquimo people who intended living there for the following winter were landed. A very large supply of meat was landed also; in addition to the meat quite a number of useful presents, hatchets, knives, needles, some boards for the making and repairing of sledges, and some wood for lance- and harpoon-staves, and a box full of soap were landed. This inventory of presents may seem cheap and paltry to you, but to these natives such presents as we made were more appreciated than the gift of many dollars would be by a poverty-stricken family in this country. With the materials that Commander Peary furnished would be made the weapons of the chase, the tools of the seamstress, and the implements of the homemaker. The Esquimos have always known how to utilize every factor furnished by nature, and what has been given to them by the Commander has been given with the simple idea of helping them to make their life easier, and proves again the axiom, "The Lord helps those who help themselves."

After disembarking the Karnah contingent, the ship steamed to Etah, arriving there on the afternoon of August 17. As the *Roosevelt* was entering the harbor of Etah, all hands were on deck and on the lookout, for it was here that we were again to come in touch with the world we had left behind a year before. A large number of Esquimos were running up and down the shore, but there was no sign of the expected ship. Quickly a boat was lowered, and I saw to it that I was a member of the crew of that boat, and when we reached the beach the first person to greet me was old Panikpah, greasy, smiling, and happy as if I were his own son. I quickly recognized my old friend Pooadloonah, who greeted me with a merry laugh, and my misgivings as to the fate of this precious pair were dispelled. If you will remember, Panikpah and Pooadloonah were the two Esquimos who found, when on our Pole-ward journey, just about the time we had struck the Big Lead, that there were a couple of fox-traps, or something like that, that they had forgotten to attend to, and that it was extremely necessary for them to go back and square up their accounts. Here they were, fat, smiling, and healthy; and I apprehend somewhat surprised to see us, but they bluffed it out well.

Murphy and the young man Pritchard were also here, Murphy and Pritchard were the members of the crew who had been left here to guard the provisions of the expedition, and to trade with the Esquimos. Another person also was there to greet us; but who had kept himself alive and well by his own pluck and clear grit, and who reported on meeting the Commander of having had a most satisfactory and enjoyable experience. I refer to Mr. Harry Whitney, the young man from New Haven, Conn., who had elected at the last hour, the previous autumn, to remain at Etah, to hunt the big game of the region. When the *Roosevelt* had sailed north from Etah, the previous August, he had been left absolutely alone; the *Erik* had sailed for home, and there was no way out of this desolate land for him until the relief ship came north the following year, or the *Roosevelt* came south to take him aboard. His outfit and equipment were sufficient for him and complete, but he had shared it with the natives until it was exhausted, and after that he had reverted to the life of the aborigines. When the *Roosevelt* reached Etah, Mr. Whitney was an Esquimo; but within one hour, he had a bath, a shave, and a hair-cut, and was the same mild-mannered gentleman that we had left there in the fall. He had gratified his ambitions in shooting musk-oxen, but he had not killed a single polar bear.

At Etah there were two boys, Etookahshoo and Ahpellah, boys about sixteen or seventeen years old, who had been with Dr. Cook for a year, or ever since he had crossed the channel to Ellesmere Land and returned again. These boys are the two he claims accompanied him to the North Pole. To us, up there at Etah, such a story was so ridiculous and absurd that we simply laughed at it. We knew Dr. Cook and his abilities; he had been the surgeon on two of Peary's expeditions and, aside from his medical ability, we had no faith in him whatever. He was not even good for a day's work, and the idea of his making such an astounding claim as having reached the Pole was so ludicrous that, after our laugh, we dropped the matter altogether.

On account of the world-wide controversy his story has caused, I will quote from my diary the impressions noted in regard to him:

"August 17, 1909, Etah, North Greenland.

"Mr. Harry Whitney came aboard with the boatswain and the cabin-boy, who had been left here last fall on our way to Cape Sheridan. Murphy is the boatswain and Pritchard the boy, both from Newfoundland, and they look none the worse for wear, in spite of the long time they have spent here. Mr. Whitney is the gentleman who came upon the *Erik* last year, and at the last moment decided to spend the winter with the natives. He had a long talk with the Commander before we left for the north, and has had quite a lengthy session with him since. I learn that Dr. Cook came over from Ellesmere Land with his two boys, Etookahshoo and Ahpellah, and in a confidential conversation with Mr. Whitney made the statement that he had reached the North Pole. Professor MacMillan and I have talked to his two boys and have learned that there is no foundation in fact for such a statement, and the Captain and others of the expedition have questioned them, and if they were out on the ice of the Arctic Ocean it was only for a very short distance, not more than twenty or twenty-five miles. The boys are positive in this statement, and my own boys, Ootah and Ooqueah, have talked to them also, and get the same replies. It is a fact that they had a very hard time and were reduced to low limits, but they have not been any distance north, and the Commander and the rest of us are in the humor to regard Mr. Whitney as a person who has been hoodwinked. We know Dr. Cook very well and also his reputation, and we know that he was never good for a hard day's work; in fact he was not up to the average, and he is no hand at all in making the most of his resources. He probably has spun this yarn to Mr. Whitney and the boatswain to make himself look big to them.

"The Commander will not permit Mr. Whitney to bring any of the Dr. Cook effects aboard the *Roosevelt* and they have been left in a cache on shore. Koolootingwah is here again, after his trip to North Star Bay with Dr. Cook, and tells an amusing story of his experience."

It is only from a sense of justice to Commander Peary and those who were with him that I have mentioned Dr. Cook. The outfitting of the hunting expedition of Mr. Bradley was well known to us. Captain Bartlett had directed it and had advised and arranged for the purchase of the Schooner *John R. Bradley* to carry the hunting party to the region where big game of the character Mr. Bradley wished to hunt could be found. We knew that Dr. Cook was accompanying Mr. Bradley, but we had no idea that the question of the discovery of the North Pole was to be involved.

I have reason to be grateful to Dr. Cook for favors received; I lived with his folks while I was suffering with my eyes, due to snow blindness, but I feel that all of the debts of gratitude have been liquidated by my silence in this controversy, and I will have nothing more to say in regard to him or to his claims.

CHAPTER XXI

Etah to New York—Coming of Mail and Reporters—Home!

At Etah we expected to meet the relief ship. Sixty tons of coal and a small quantity of provisions had been left there during the previous summer, to be used by us on our homeward voyage. This coal was loaded on board and the Esquimos who desired to remain at Etah were landed. Just at the time we were ready to sail a heavy storm of wind and snow blew up, and it was not until six P.M. on the 20th that we left the harbor. Farewells had been said to the Esquimos, all that had been promised them for faithful services had been given to them, and we commenced the final stage of our journey home.

From Etah, August 20, the ship sailed along the coast, landing Esquimos at the different settlements, and on the 23rd of August at two A.M., we met the Schooner *Jeanie,* of St. John, N.F., commanded by Samuel Bartlett. The schooner was supplied with provisions and coal for the relief of the *Roosevelt,* and was executing the plan of the Peary Arctic Club.

There was mail aboard her and we had our first tidings of home and friends in a twelve-month. From newspaper clippings I learned that the British Antarctic Expedition, commanded by Sir Ernest H. Shackleton, had reached within 111 miles of the South Pole.

The mail contained good news for all but one of us. Mr. Borup, in his bunk above the Professor's, read his letters, and in the course of his reading was heard to emit a deep sigh, then to utter an agonizing groan. Prof. MacMillan, thinking that Borup had received bad news indeed, endeavored to console him, and at the same time asked what was the bad news, feeling sure it could be nothing less than the death of Colonel Borup or some other close relative of his.

"What is the matter, George? Tell me."

"HARVARD BEAT YALE!"

The *Roosevelt,* accompanied by her consort, sailed south to North Star Bay and while entering the harbor ran ashore. Late in the afternoon, however, the rising tide floated her. While waiting for the tide, a party of six, I among the number, went ashore and visited the Danish Missionary settlement established there, the Esquimos acting as our interpreters, we being unable to speak Danish and the missionaries being unable to speak English. It was in North Star Bay that the coal and provisions from the *Jeanie* were transferred to the *Roosevelt.*

Aboard the *Jeanie,* there was a young Esquimo man, Mene, who for the past twelve years had lived in New York City, but, overcome by a strong desire to live again in his own country, had been sent north by his friends in the States. He was almost destitute, having positively nothing in the way of equipment to enable him to withstand the rigors of the country, and was no more fitted for the life he was to take up than any boy of eighteen or twenty would be, for he was but a little boy when he first left North Greenland. However, Commander Peary ordered that he be given a plentiful supply of furs to keep him warm, food, ammunition and loading outfit, traps and guns, but, I believe, he would have gladly returned with us, for it was a wistful farewell he made, and an Esquimo's farewell is usually very barren of pathos.

Mr. Whitney transferred his augmented equipment to the *Jeanie,* intending to remain with her down the Labrador, for her Captain had agreed to use every effort to help Mr. Whitney secure at least one polar bear.

Cape York was reached on the morning of August 25, and from the two Esquimo families, living at the extreme point of the Cape, we obtained the mail which had been left there by Captain Adams of the Dundee Whaling Fleet *Morning Star*. Our letters, although they bore no more recent a date than that of March 23, 1909, were eagerly read.

At Cape York we landed the last of the Esquimos. The decks were now cleared. The boats were securely lashed in their davits, and nine A.M., August 26, in a gale of wind, the *Roosevelt* put out to sea, homeward-bound, but not yet out of danger, for the gale increased so considerably that the *Roosevelt* was forced to lay to under reefed foresail, in the lee of the middle pack, until the 29th, when the storm subsided and the ship got under way again.

On September 4 the Labrador was sighted. Under full steam we passed the Farmyard, a group of small islands which lie off the coast.

We arrived at Turnavik at seven-thirty P.M. Once again we saw signs of civilization. The men and women appeared in costumes of the Twentieth Century instead of the fur garments of the Esquimos. Here we loaded nineteen tons of coal. Here we feasted on fresh codfish, fresh vegetables, and other appetizing foods to which our palates had long been strangers.

You know the rest, for from Turnavik to Indian Harbor was only a few hours' sailing.

At Indian Harbor was located the wireless telegraph station from where Commander Peary flashed to the civilized world his laconic message, "Stars and Stripes nailed to the North Pole."

Within half an hour of our arrival, the British cutter *Fiona* entered the harbor and the officers came aboard the *Roosevelt.* Thereafter for every hour there was continuous excitement and reception of visitors.

On September 13th the steamer *Douglas H. Thomas,* of Sydney, C.B., arrived, having on board two representatives of the Associated Press, accompanied by Mr. Rood, a representative of *Harper's Magazine.*

The next day the cable-boat *Tyrian* arrived, with seventeen newspaper reporters, five photographers, and one stenographer. The *Tyrian* anchored outside the harbor and in five life-boats the party was brought aboard the *Roosevelt.* As they rowed they cheered, and when they sighted Commander Peary three ringing cheers and a tiger were given. The newspapermen requested an interview with the Commander. He granted their request, at the same time suggesting that they accompany him ashore to a fish-loft at the end of the pier, where there would be more room than aboard the ship. Accompanied by the members of the expedition, the Commander and the reporters left the ship. Arriving at the loft Commander Peary sat on some fish-nets at the rear end of the loft, some of the reporters sat on barrels and nets, others squatted on the floor. They formed a semi-circle around him and eagerly listened to the first telling of his stirring story.

Before leaving Battle Harbor, we received a visit from the great missionary, Dr. Grenfell, the effect of whose presence was almost like a benediction.

On the morning of the 18th we left Battle Harbor accompanied by the tug *Douglas H. Thomas,* amidst the salutes of the many vessels and boats in the harbor and the cannon on the hill.

Through the Straits of Belle Isle we steamed, with a fair wind and a choppy sea. In the meantime I was busily engaged in making a strip to sew upon a large American flag. This was a broad white bar which was to extend from the upper right to the lower left corner of the flag, with the words "North Pole" sewed on it.

About six A.M. on the 21st, a large white, steam-yacht was seen approaching, flying an American flag from her foremast and the English flag from the mizzenmast. We were close enough to her to distinguish Mrs. Peary and the children on board. A boat was quickly lowered from the yacht and the Peary family was soon united aboard the *Roosevelt.*

All kinds of sailing craft now met the *Roosevelt* and by them she was escorted into the harbor of Sydney, C.B. Whistles were blown, thousands of people lined the shores of the harbor, cheering enthusiastically and waving flags, and as the *Roosevelt* was moored alongside the pier, a delegation of schoolgirls met the Commander, made an address, and presented him with a magnificent bouquet. The streets were gorgeously decorated and a holiday had been declared. A ripe, royal welcome was accorded the *Roosevelt* and the members of the expedition. Visitors boarded the ship and looted successfully for souvenirs.

It was at Sydney that the expedition commenced to disband. Commander Peary and his family returned to the United States via railroad-train.

The *Roosevelt* left Sydney on September 22 for New York City. A stop was made at Eagle Island, in Casco Bay, off the coast of Maine, where is located the summer home of Commander Peary, and here we landed most of his paraphernalia, some sledges and dogs. From Eagle Island we steamed direct to Sandy Hook, reaching there at noon on October 2. The next day the *Roosevelt* took her place with the replica of those two historic ships, the *Half Moon* and the *Clermont,* in the lead of the great naval parade.

And now my story is ended; it is a tale that is told. "Now is Othello's occupation gone."

I long to see them all again! the brave, cheery companions of the trail of the North. I long to see again the lithe figure of my Commander! and to hear again his clear, ringing voice urging and encouraging me onward, with his "Well done, my boy." I want to be with the party when they reach the untrod shores of Crocker Land; I yearn to be with those who reach the South Pole, the lure of the Arctic is tugging at my heart, to me the trail is calling!

"The Old Trail!
The Trail that is always New!"

APPENDIX I

Notes on the Esquimos

THE ORIGIN OF THE ESQUIMOS is not known to a certainty. In color they are brown, their hair is heavy, straight, coarse, and black. In appearance they are short, fat, and well-developed; and they bear a strong resemblance to the Mongolian race.

Among the men of this tribe, quarrels and fights very rarely occur; but it is a very noticeable fact that while the men of the tribe do not make war on each other, the man of the family will, at the least provocation on the part of his better-half, without hesitation apply brute force to show his authority.

The tribe of these, the North Greenland Esquimos, numbers two hundred and eighteen.

Great interest was shown by the men when working implements, such as we used on board ship, were shown them. Eagerly they listened while the uses of many of these tools were explained to them. The women also showed great interest in any article that was foreign to them. They have a special liking for fancy beads of the smaller variety.

The Esquimos show a great capacity for imitation. They have also a marked sense of humor.

An Esquimo's sense of imitation is so keen that it is only necessary for him to observe a sledge-maker at work but once, when the same type of sledge will be reproduced in a very short time. On my last trip north, I noticed that the shirts worn by the Esquimos were similar in style and cut to our own. In 1906, the style had been entirely different.

The Esquimos show no desire to acquire the English language. With the exception of Kudlooktoo and Inighito, none of the tribe could speak English intelligently. The Esquimos' vocabulary is a complication of prefixes and suffixes, and many words in his language are very hard to pronounce.

The *tupiks* (tents) are made of sealskin, and are used in summer. The igloos are built of snow, and are used in winter. A few igloos built of bowlders can be seen. The workmanship of this latter type of igloos is necessarily crude, for the bowlders are used in the rough state. On entering the *tuscoonah* (entrance), a bed-platform of stones five feet long, and six feet wide, confronts one. On each side of this platform are seen smaller platforms, each holding a *koodlah* (fire-pot).

This *koodlah* is made of a stone so soft that before it comes in contact with fire it can easily be cut with a knife. The name given by the Esquimos to it is *okeyoah*. Cooking utensils are first formed in the desired shape, then heat is applied, as a result of which the stone quickly hardens. The method of cooking as employed by the Esquimos is to suspend the *kooleesoo* (cooking-pot) over the *koodlah* (fire-pot). The *koodlah* is the only means by which light can be secured in an Esquimo igloo. As fuel, the blubber of the narwhal is used.

The clothing of the male Esquimo consists of a *kooletah* (deerskin coat with hood attached) *nanookes* (foxskin trousers) and *kamiks* (sealskin boots); that of the female Esquimo, a *kopetah* (foxskin coat with hood attached) *nanookes* (foxskin trousers) and hip length *kamiks* (sealskin boots). The shirts of the male and female Esquimo are made from the skin of the auks, and one hundred and fifty of these little birds are used in the manufacture of one shirt.

The largest Esquimo family known among the North Greenland tribe, numbers six; as a rule, an Esquimo family rarely outnumbers three. An Esquimo family is not stationary. Rarely does a family remain in one place longer than one season, which is nine months. The principal reason for this constant moving is the scarcity of game; for after a season of hunting in one place, game becomes very scarce; and there is no other alternative but for the family to move on. Transportation is by means of sledges drawn by a team of dogs. Alcoholic drinks are not known among this tribe; but, of late, tobacco is extensively used. Previous to 1902, before the arrival of the Danes, tobacco was an unknown quantity.

The cleanliness of the Esquimos leaves room for much improvement.

With reference to their morals, strictly speaking they are markedly lax. The wife of an Esquimo is held in no higher esteem than are the goods and chattels of the household. She may at any time be loaned, borrowed, sold, or exchanged. They have no marriage ceremony.

The amusements of the Esquimos are few. Tests of strength and endurance occur between the men of the tribe; and visits are paid to the various settlements, during the long winter nights; and songs and choruses are sung, accompanied by a kind of tambourine which is made from the bladder of a walrus or seal, and stretched across the antlers of a reindeer.

The Esquimos are a very superstitious people. In the event of a fatal illness, the victim, just before death, is removed to a place outside the igloo, for should death enter the igloo that dwelling would instantly be destroyed. If the deceased be a man, he is rolled up in a sealskin, and strips of rawhide are lashed around the body to keep the skin intact. He is then carried to his last resting place. A low stone structure is built around the body to protect it from the foxes. His sledge, containing all his belongings, is placed close beside this structure, and his dogs harnessed to his sledge are strangled, and stretched their full length, with the forepaws extended. In the event of the deceased being a woman, her cooking utensils are placed beside her, and should she be the mother of a very young infant, its life is taken. In the case of a widower, the bereaved Esquimo remains in the igloo for three days, during which time a new suit of wearing apparel is made, and worn by him, and all clothing made by the deceased is, by him, destroyed. His term of mourning now being ended, the Esquimo, without more ado, takes unto himself a new wife. Members of the tribe who have the same name as the deceased have to change that name until the arrival of a new-born babe, to whom the name is given, whereby the ban is removed. The Esquimos have no decided form of religion. When questioned as to where the soul of the good Esquimo will go, they reply by pointing upward; and by pointing downward, the question is answered as to the final dwelling-place of the wicked.

The main cause of death amongst the Esquimos is from a disease the symptoms of which are a cough, nausea, and fever, which disease quickly causes death.

It is true that the Esquimos are of little value to the commercial world, due probably to their isolated position; but these same unlearned and uncivilized people have rendered valuable assistance in the discovery of the North Pole.

APPENDIX II

List of Smith Sound Esquimos

(Males marked by an asterisk)

Ac-com-o-ding′-wah*
Ah-ding′-ah-loo
Ah-dul-ah-ko-tee′-ah*
Ah-dul-ah-ko-tee′-ah*
Ah-ga-tah′
Ah-go′-tah*
Ah-kah-gee′-ah-how
A-ka-ting′-wah
A-ka-ting′-wah
Ah-li-kah-sing′-wah
Ah-li-kah-sing′-wah
Ah-li-kah-sing′-wah
Ah′-mah
Ah-mame′-ee
Ah-mo-ned′-dy
Ah-mung′-wah
Ah-nad′-doo
Ah-nah′-we
Ah-nah-wing′-wah
Ahng-een′-yah*
Ahng-een′-yah
Ahng′-ing-nah
Ahng-ma-lok′to*
Ahng-nah′-nia
Ahng-no-ding′-wah
Ahng-o-do-blah′-o*
Ahng-o-di-gip′-so
Ahng′-od-loo*
Ah-ni-ghi′-to
Ah-ni-ghi′-to
Ah-ning′-wah
Ah-ning′-wah
Ah-now′-kah*
Ah-now′-kay*
Ah′-pel-lah*
Ah′-pel-lah*
Ah-pud-ding′-wah*
Ah-say′-oo*
Ah′-te-tah

Ah′-te-tah
Ah-took-sung′-wah
Ah-tung′-ee-nah
Ah-tung′-ee-nah
Ah-wa-ting′-wah*
Ah-wa-tok′-suah*
Ah-wee′-ah
Ah-wee′-ah
Ah-wee-ah-good′-loo
Ah-wee-aung-o′-nah
Ah-wee′-i-ah*
Ah-we-ging′-wah*
Ah-we-shung′-wah*
Ah-wok-tun′-ee-ah
Ak-pood-ah-shah′-o*
Ak-pood-ah-shah′-o*
Ak-pood′-ee-ark*
Ak-pood-e-uk′-ee
A-le′-tah*
Al′-nay-ah
Al-nay-du′-ah
Ar-ke′-o*
Ar-ke′-o*
Ar-ke′-o*

E-gee′-ah*
E-ging′-wah*
E-ging′-wah*
E-lay-ting′-wah
E-ling′-wah*
E-meen′-yah*
E-she-a′-too
E-shing′-wah
E-tood′-loo*
E-took′-ah-shoo*
E-took′-ah-shoo*
E-too-shok′-swah
E′-vah-loo
E′-vah-loo
E′-we

I-ah-ping′-wah*
I-ah-ping′-wah*
Ig-lood-ee-ark′-swee*
Ihr′-lee*
Ik′-wah*
Ik-kile-e-oo′-shah
Il-kah-lin′-ah
Il-kli-ah′*
Il-kli-ah′*
In-ad-lee′-ah
In-ad-lee′-ah
In′-ah-loo
In-it-ghi′-to*
In-it-ghi′-to*
In-it-ghi′-to*
In-noo′-i-tah*
In-noo-tah′
In-noo-tah′
In-u-ah-pud′-o*
In-u-ah′-o
In-yah-lung′-wah
I-on′-ah
I-o-wit′-ty*

Jacok-su′-nah*

Kah′-dah*
Kah-ko-tee′-ah
Kah-ko-tee′-ah*
Kah-shad′-doo
Kah-shoo′-be-doo*

Kai-o-ang′-wah*
Kai-o-ang′-wah*
Kai′-oh*
Kai-o-look′-to*
Kai-o′-tah*
Kai-we-ark′-shah*
Kai-we-ing′-wah*
Kai′-we-kah*
Kai-ung′-wah*
Kang-nah′*
Kes-shoo′*
Ke-shung′-wah*
Klay′-oo
Klay′-oo
Klay-ung′-wah
Klip-e-sok′-swah*
Kood′-ee-puck
Kood-loo-tin′-ah*
Kood-loo-tin′ah*
(or Koolatoonah)
Koo-e-tig′-e-to*
Koo′-lee
Kool-oo-ting′-wah*
Koo-u-pee′
Koo-u-pee′
Kud′-ah-shah*
Kud′-lah*
Kud′-lah*
Kud-lun′-ah*
Kud-look′-too*
Ky-u-tah*

Ma-gip′-soo
Mah-so′-nah*
Mah-so′-nah*
Mah-so′-nah*
Mah-so′-nah*
Mark-sing′-wah*
Mee′-tik*
Mee′-tik*
Me-gip′-soo
Mek′-kah
Me′-ne*
Merk-to-shah′*
Mok′-sah*
Mok-sang′-wah
Mok-sang′-wah
Mon′-nie
Mon′-nie
Micky′-shoo
My′-ah*
My-o′-tah*

Nay-dee-ing′-wah
Nel-lee′-kah
Nel-lee-ka-tee′-ah
Net′-too
Net′-too
New-e-king′-wah
New-e-king′-wah
New-e-king′-wah
New-hate′-e-lah′-o*
New-hate′-e-lah′-o*
New-kah-ping′-wah*
Nip-sang′-wah*
Now-o-yat′-loe
Nup′-sah

Og′-we*
Oo-ah-oun′*
Oo-bloo′-yah*
Oo-bloo′-yah*
Oo′-mah*

Oo-que′-ah*
Oo′-tah*
Oo-tun′-iah
Oo-we′-ah-oop*
Oo-we-she-a′-too

Pan′-ik-pah*
Pee-ah-wah′-to*
Poo-ad-loo′-nah*
Poo-ad-loo′-nah*
Poo-ad-loo′-nah*
Poob′-lah*
Poob′-lah*
Pood-lung′-wah
Poo′-too

Sag′-wah
Sat′-too*
Seeg′-loo*
Seen-o-ung′-wah
See-o-dee-kah′-to
Shoo-e-king′-wah
Sim′-e-ah
Sin-ah′-ew
Sip′-soo
Sow′-nah
Suk′-kun*
Sul-ming′-wah*

Tah′-tah-rah*
Tah′-wah-nah*
Taw-ching′-wah*
Taw-ching′-wah*
Teddy-ilng′-wah*
Toi-tee′-ah*
Took-e-ming′-wah
Too′-koom-ah
Tu-bing′-wah
Tung-wing′-wah
Tung′-we*

Ung′-ah*

We′-ark
We-shark′-oup-si*

Two female babies not named

Male	122
Female	96
Total	**218**

This extremely rare article was published in the *Boston American* in 1910 and may only exist as a sole copy on microfilm at the Boston Public Library. It sheds a different light on the events surrounding the discovery of the Pole.

APPENDIX III

Matt Henson Tells the Real Story of Peary's Trip to Pole

NEGRO COMPANION ADDS TO HISTORY
SAYS TOP WAS REACHED BY ERROR
THINKS HE WAS TREATED UNFAIRLY
ESKIMOS ONLY TO SHARE HONORS
PERIL OF LAST DAY'S TRAVEL RELATED
U.S. FLAG RUN UP ON HOE HANDLE
HAPPY GROUP IN A WILD LAND CHEERS
HOW DR. COOK FOOLED THE PEOPLE

THE DISCOVERY OF THE *North Pole by Commander Peary (who on his retirement assumed the rank of captain), and Matt Henson is a wonderful tale from any angle. Peary has lectured and written upon it, almost ignoring Henson, his Negro companion. Henson is even now lecturing upon it at Wonderland Park with slides, sledges, furs and polar outfit. Each tells his straightforward tale of reaching "the big nail" on top of the earth and the details of hardship and hair-breadth escapes are secondary in the weird glamour of the exploit. But there are side lights upon the journey to the Pole that have been scarcely touched upon by either lecturer. In a recent written article Commander Peary treated his former companion in a way that Henson does not like. Henson has replied by writing for the* Boston Sunday American *some of the side lights upon Commander Peary. He makes clear things long kept in the background touching the polar discovery, tells of a change of heart that came over Commander Peary when he found that they had traveled too fast and were already at the Pole. Henson says Peary intended to visit the Pole entirely alone, or accompanied only by his Esquimo boys. He also shows how impossible was the story of Dr. Cook. Henson adds that Commander Peary, in spite of his recent unkind attitude was formerly one of the best of men to work for, treats of the fortitude of those engaged in the expedition, and for the first time relates how Commander Peary rode on sledges almost all the way to the Pole and back for the very good reason that ten years before, after a similar expedition, he suffered the amputation of nine of his ten toes, a fact that, if generally known has by most people been long ago forgotten.*

By Matt Henson

Copyright 1910 by Boston American

AFTER TWENTY-TWO long years of service with Peary we are now as strangers. Three times in his company I crossed the "Great Lead" north of Cape Columbia on my way towards the Pole, and three times we recrossed together. The last round trip was the successful one. The North Pole was reached. Three hearty American cheers were given for Old Glory as we waved from an icy pinnacle. It was the culmination of a struggle lasting all those years, in which Commander Peary, the employer, and I, plain Matt Henson, the servant, had worked and starved and frozen together. From the moment I declared to Commander Peary that I believed we stood upon the Pole he apparently ceased to be my friend.

I could never understand it and cannot now. He was an exact but very kind man in authority. He was never understandable.

On the evening of the fifth day after Captain Bartlett willingly turned back with his little division of Eskimo dogs and sledges, we encamped practically at the Pole. I, who had walked, knew that we had made exceptional distances in those five days. So did the Eskimos, for they also had walked. Lieutenant Peary was the only surprised man. He, because of his crippled feet, had ridden on the sledges the greater part of the journey up, as he did upon the return. Riding, one cannot so well judge of distance traversed. He made no observation in the five days, merely knew we had 132 miles to go and he supposed that we could nearly make it in the five days of marching.

Eskimo Boy Discloses Peary's Plan

WHEN WE WENT into camp on the evening of the fifth day, actually the sixth day of April, one of my Eskimo boys—I could talk their language—spoke sneeringly to one of Commander Peary. He said it was mean that Peary had quietly planned with him and one other Eskimo boy to leave me in camp the following morning and go off to the Pole by himself. It was mean, said the young native, because we were all so near, and I had worked so hard to make the trip a success.

It stunned me at first, because Commander Peary had spoken nothing of it to me. My first impulse was to protest, but on second thought I decided to wait. In fact, I believed that the full distance had already been covered. One can tell to within a mile or so how far he walks in that northern ice, and I reckoned that we were even now at the very Pole.

Found Themselves at the North Pole

TRUE ENOUGH, on the following morning Commander Peary set out with the two Eskimos and one sledge with a tin of pemmican and instruments, leaving me repairing a sledge and in charge of the camp. I was sorely disappointed, but somehow I had an abiding faith that he was wrong in his calculations. In about an hour the Commander returned. His face was long and serious. He would not speak to me. I quietly learned from the boys accompanying him that he had made observations a few miles further on.

"Well, Mr. Peary," I spoke up, cheerfully enough, "we are now at the Pole, are we not?" "I do not suppose that we can swear we are exactly at the Pole" was his evasive answer. "Well, I have kept track of the distance and we have made exceptional time," I replied, "and I have a feeling that we have just about covered the 132 miles since Captain Bartlett turned back. If we have not traveled in the right direction then it is your own fault."

Commander Peary made no reply, but going off by himself made three separate observations. I can make observations myself, but of course, I did not meddle at this time. At the conclusion of his tests he ordered out the American flag, selected a hillock of ice and gave the word to erect the Stars and Stripes thereon. With the assistance of the native boys I did this. Then I led in a cheer for Old Glory. We remained in the encampment for about thirty-three hours when word was given for the return.

From the time we knew we were at the Pole Commander Peary scarcely spoke to me. Probably he did not speak to me four times on the whole return journey to the ship. I thought this over and it grieved me much.

I thought of the years we had worked together for the great aim. I remembered his many acts of kindness and naturally I did not forget what I had done for him. One never does that in summing up to strike a balance of friendship.

Was Peary Offended?

IT CAME OVER ME that possibly he had taken offence at us on the journey up because so frequently we kept ahead or just out of his reach so that he might not load himself upon our sledges. He was very heavy for the dogs to haul. We wanted him to remain in his own division. We knew he could walk but little in rough ice. Only one of his little toes remained from that terrible frosting of 1900. He was compelled to ride. But we did not court his presence. Much of my work was ahead of the main party breaking the trail and caring for advance things.

I wondered if he remembered with any gratitude those awful days in 1900 when he lost his toes and became a cripple on my hands. Those were days that even now stand out from all the rest. How I kept the men and dogs in order, traveling days and during the night how I foraged with the dogs, like a dog myself, hunting for food to keep him alive and get him back to civilization. We hunted and captured any living thing that was good to eat, chase hares with wolfish desperation, and I finally saw him back to the ship in the hands of the surgeon, crippled for life in a way, but safe and eventually well.

It nearly broke my heart on the journey from the Pole that he would arise in the morning and slip away on the homeward trail without rapping on the ice for me, as was the established custom. As we approached our goal he vouchsafed a few words in effect that he hurry on ahead, losing one nights sleep, while I could bring the party in at my leisure.

Did Not Say Good-by

ON BOARD the ship he addressed me a very few times. When we left the ship he did not speak. I wrote to him twice and sent a telegram, but received no reply from him.

I had worked for Commander Peary all those years for the sum of $35 a month and found, until this last trip, when I received $50 a month and keep, and I had scarcely enough money to support my family in the States. In my letters I hoped for some understanding.

But no reply came until I was signed for a series of lectures. When I had given my first lecture I received a telegram from Commander Peary warning me not to use the pictures. At once I sat down and wrote him another long letter. He never replied to it. I have kept my lectures and illustrations.

And bear in mind that all the pictures were taken by me. Besides those I am now exhibiting I exposed 110 films about the Pole which, upon his request, I loaned to Commander Peary. It was my camera. I paid for the films, exposed and developed them. He borrowed the films saying he would use some and return them to me. He has never done this and for all I know has my 110 films in his possession.

Peary's Great Disappointment

IT WAS MY BOY O-tah who disclosed to me that Peary was to leave me behind in the final few miles to the Pole, and with E-tig-wah he witnesses the disappointment of Commander Peary when a few miles from the camp, his observation told the lieutenant that he had overstepped and gone past the Pole, which we had reached the night before. Our camp itself was practically situated on "the top of the earth." For the crime of being present when the Pole was reached Commander Peary has ignored me ever since.

After twenty-two years of close companionship he refused even to say good-by when we separated in New York. And at Fort Conger, nearly ten years before, we had carried Peary nearly 200 miles with his feet frozen, traveling days and hunting nights for food to keep him and ourselves alive!

Captain Bartlett was glad to turn back when he did. He frankly told me several times that he had little expectation of ever returning alive. Several times he said he had gone far enough and would be "blame glad" when his time came to stop. After parting with him our trail became much easier until on the final day's march we must have made fully thirty miles, and were at our destination.

Bartlett took back two natives, eighteen dogs and one sledge. During the last five days of advance he was engaged to break the trail, but in the roughest ice I had to do it, better fitted through long polar experience.

Leaving Bartlett the morning of April 2 we made twenty miles and the second and following days we made greater distances. No observations were taken. We reached the Pole the night of April 6, when I heard that I was to be deserted on the following morning. Fortunately for me we even then "arrived." On the morning of April 7th I was surely enough deserted, but not for long. Upon his return in an hour Peary ordered out a pole, consisting of a long hoe handle, to hold up an American flag.

He gave the order to the Eskimos and did not mention any part I might take in the ceremony. I did not mind, but pitched in and led the cheering.

Cheers for the U.S. Flag

I CAN SEE NOW that we could have reached the North Pole in 1906 if we had made haste in the colder season. Instead time was wasted in establishing stations which could never be of value, because the Polar ice is always moving. The warmer season arrived and caught us and we hastened back to avoid the ever-opening "leads" of water.

You ask about Dr. Cook. No, he did not reach the Pole and he could not. I know that with all my experience I could not take two men and the equipment he said he had and get within 200 miles of the Pole. If I should reach within 250 miles of it I would be doing extremely well.

It is true that the Eskimos told me, for I obtained for Peary the details of Cook's performances, which he afterward offered as his own investigation, that Cook was not once out of sight of land. He had tried, and seeing the uselessness of it had made for Jones Sound to catch a whaler home. The ice had kept the whalers out and Cook was left upon his own resources. His Eskimo boys were in the same fix and all had to stay until conditions changed.

Cook's Mind Affected?

SOMETIMES I think it all affected Cook's mind. He wanted to reach the Pole, tried hard and thought of it so much and so greatly that at last he half hypnotized himself into the idea he had been there and then found easy credence. If Peary had let him alone until the full truth came out Cook would not have skimmed the financial cream from the North Pole situation.

Peary Only Advertised Dr. Cook

ONE CANNOT fake records to convince scientific men of a bogus trip to the North Pole. Peary need not have hurried to unmask Cook. It were much better to have allowed matters to take their course. Contrary to the belief of many, the Eskimos do not like Dr. Cook. He owed them much and paid in promises. Neither do they generally like Peary, though Peary paid his obligations. But the Eskimos who were brought to this country and who afterward denounced Peary were wrong. Peary was not responsible for their condition. Another story is involved. He brought them here, that is all. On others rests the responsibility.

The "Big Lead" Explained

THE "BIG LEAD" so often spoken of is a break in the polar ice always found north of Cape Columbia. Once it was three miles wide. We waited for "young ice" to cross it. A word for the polar dogs. They are intuitive and cunning and spread out on thin ice with an understanding almost human. When the "young ice" is yielding, elastic and wavy the dogs open out like a fan and do not break through. The men walk respectful distances from the sledges. Occasionally a sledge breaks through.

Lieutenant Peary's custom was to request rather than command. Could we do so-and-so at such a time? If we answered in the affirmative he would then hold as to an exact accomplishment of the task as per agreement.